"With humility, honesty, and authenticity, Courtney Carver invites each of us to find greater simplicity in life—and provides a practical road map for us to find it in our own unique way." —JOSHUA BECKER, founder of Becoming Minimalist and author of *The More of Less*

"*Soulful Simplicity* encourages conscious minimalism from the inside out. It's a heartfelt yet practical guide for making life simple again. Courtney's story is relatable in so many ways—she lets you walk in her shoes so you can see the mental and physical steps she took to escape a stressful life that literally almost killed her. This book has made me laugh, smile, and take action toward living a life uncluttered by most of the needless things people fill their lives with, leaving me with space for what truly matters. A life that isn't constant busyness, rushing, and stress, but instead contemplation, creation, and connection with people and projects I love." —ANGEL CHERNOFF, author and coach, Marc and Angel Hack Life

"If organizing your stuff worked, you'd be organized by now. Get this book for its strategic 'hows' and even more powerful 'whys.'" —DEREK SIVERS, sivers.org

Soulful Simplicity

HOW LIVING WITH LESS CAN LEAD TO SO MUCH MORE

Courtney Carver

A TarcherPerigee Book

tarcherperigee

An imprint of Penguin Random House LLC
375 Hudson Street
New York, New York 10014

Most TarcherPerigee books are available at special quantity discounts for
bulk purchase for sales promotions, premiums, fund-raising, and educational needs.
Special books or book excerpts also can be created to fit specific needs.
For details, write: SpecialMarkets@penguinrandomhouse.com.

Library of Congress Cataloging-in-Publication Data
Names: Carver, Courtney, author.
Title: Soulful simplicity: how living with less can lead to so much more /
by Courtney Carver.
Description: New York, New York: Tarcherperigee, [2017] | "A Tarcherperigee Book."
Identifiers: LCCN 2017024024 | ISBN 9780143130680
Subjects: LCSH: Simplicity.
Classification: LCC BJ1496 .C39 2017 | DDC 179/.9—dc23
LC record available at https://lccn.loc.gov/2017024024

Printed in the United States of America
1   3   5   7   9   10   8   6   4   2

Book design by Elke Sigal

You gave me space to breathe, time to heal,
and love, so much love.

CONTENTS

SECTION ONE

MAKING ME: I HAD TO START WITH THE INSIDE

When You Live or Work Outside of Your Heart,
There Will Always Be a Breakup, Breakdown, or Both

SECTION FOUR

MAKING LOVE: WHAT REALLY MATTERS

Simplicity Is the Way Back to Love

Wanting More

All of the things I thought were true about my life changed during one phone call that lasted less than five minutes. When I picked up the phone in my cubicle at work and heard "You have MS," the only thing I could think was "This can't be true." I never thought I'd be diagnosed with an incurable disease that threatened my health, my active lifestyle, my family, and my work. I never thought I'd get a wake-up call I couldn't ignore. Then again, I never considered the possibility of being debt-free, clutter-free, mostly stress-free, or doing work that gives my life enormous purpose either.

Back to the wake-up call for a moment. Whoever hands out wake-up calls must have known they would have to deliver a big one to get my attention. The whispers and gentle nudges hadn't worked, but multiple sclerosis? Now I was listening. I hadn't been listening for a long time, not to my body, my heart, or my soul. Instead, I was just reacting. I was reacting to everything thrown my way, and going through the motions simply to keep up with life's demands, and to honor the vow I had made almost a decade before to always give my daughter more.

The Breakup

I was married to someone who didn't love me, who couldn't love me . . . for seven years. Some of the worst things that have ever happened to me happened in that marriage, but some of the very best things too. For instance, were it not for my first marriage, my daughter, the person who means more to me than anyone, wouldn't be a part of my life. Another benefit of my first marriage is that after being in it, I was so sure about what I did not want in my life anymore. I didn't want to be sad, scared, or worried all the time. I wasn't exactly sure what I did want, but I knew it was more than that.

There were the negatives too: the mean words, the alcoholism, the distrust, and the feeling of immense failure. The verbal assaults, constant drinking, lying, and overspending were bad, but it was the complete disregard for my heart that in the end *was* the end. On the day my daughter was born, I was changing her first diaper, hours after an emergency C-section, and I realized I couldn't reach a new diaper without leaving her side. I asked my husband to help, and his response was something like "Jesus, get it together. You need to know how to do this when I'm not around." As he rolled his eyes, I thought to myself, "Oh, I will." In that moment, I silently vowed to give my daughter more one day.

There were more conversations that broke my heart right up until our last. After he moved out, I thought we could begin to heal. I wanted him to have a relationship with our daughter, but after picking her up from a visit and seeing beer cans roll out from under the driver's seat of his car, I sought supervised visits. The courts denied my request and said he had a right to defend himself. The last time I saw him he said, "I wish you would die so

I could raise her on my own." I could smell the beer on his breath and see the disgust in his eyes. I didn't care what the courts said anymore. He had never physically hurt me before, but I was done taking chances. I had to protect my daughter, my heart, and my life.

When I finally walked away, my only legal win was sole custody of my daughter. It was all I wanted. I assumed responsibility for almost everything else. I just didn't care. She was all that mattered. I was deeper in debt, legal fees, and uncertainty than ever before, but I held on tight to my vow to give her more. I would give her everything. I'd work harder, make more, buy her more, do more for her, and prove to her that everything would be okay. I had no idea that this new goal would be just as damaging, and just as hard on my heart.

Just the Two of Us

Once I was on my own, I had to figure out how to make ends meet. I was working full time making $17,000 a year, and my daughter was in day care full time. I wasn't receiving child support and wasn't going to chase it and invite the madness back. I was paying more than $1,100 a month in child care and rent and making just over $1,400. Add the utilities, groceries, clothes, insurance, and a car payment and all that's left over is the credit card. I wanted the first Christmas on our own to be special. Each Christmas from my childhood was grander than the last, filled with more and more presents, and I wanted to be sure my daughter had the same experience. I didn't have the money for one gift, let alone piles of presents, so I applied for every store credit card I could think of. My credit cards were close to their limits, but if I could find a few hundred dollars of credit at a few stores, I thought I could give my daughter the Christmas she deserved. What was I thinking? At three years old, she couldn't possibly enjoy the on-slaught of gifts, and by January 1 my spending hangover set in. Things had to change.

I applied for financial assistance through the state but made a little too much money to qualify. They suggested I quit my job to take advantage of what they had to offer, but that was never an option for me. Instead, I found a new job that, while much more demanding, paid considerably more. With it came my first cell phone, and my first commission check. I had arrived. The more I worked, the more I made, and the more I spent . . . and I wanted even more.

My commissions were paid quarterly, and with that influx of cash, the last thing I wanted to do was pay extra on my credit cards. Instead, I took my daughter shopping. We went out to eat and did all of the things that weren't available to us for a while. We went to Club Med—twice—and lots of other places too. I was working so hard and had put up with so much. So I thought we deserved more.

Spoiler alert: While I could never have articulated it then, I did want more—more love, connection, laughter, and adventure. All that was too hard to measure, so instead I made more money, worked more, spent more, and accumulated more.

And Then There Were Three

I met my husband Mark when I turned thirty. If you believe in soul mates, I would call him mine. When we went on our first date, Bailey cried as I left her with my mom, who was visiting. When he asked, "Why don't we bring her along?" I knew he could be my man because he already cared about my heart and hers. His sister introduced us, and after our first date, I told her I wasn't sure if it was a date thing or a friend thing. That evening after our conversation, Mark sent me an e-mail with the subject line: *Date*. In his e-mail, he listed all the definitions of the word *date* he could find, from fruit to appointments to romantic get-togethers. He said he'd be happy to take me on another date to clear up any confusion I had. That was the beginning of our love story.

Many of our first dates had been mountain hikes, overnight adventures at Appalachian Mountain Club huts in New England, or arriving first at ski resorts for early morning runs. Ninety percent of those dates included Bailey. We were all getting to know one another, and it didn't take long before I fell in love with both the man and the trails. Hiking, skiing, and other adventures became the core of our relationship. After six years of getting to know each other and falling in love in New Hampshire, we moved to Utah to live closer to my parents and the mountains that had stolen our hearts while visiting, and got married. The night after Mark proposed to me, he proposed to Bailey. He gave her a small box with his grandmother's ring inside. He had the ring engraved *jag älskar dig*, which means "I love you" in Swedish. He included a small note in the box that read, "Will you be my daughter?" We were excited for new adventures in the Utah mountains and to start our lives together as a family. We had good paying jobs, bought a big house with a yard, garage, attic, and storage shed. We bought new furniture, a new car, and all the stuff we thought we needed to be happy. We wanted it all. Then one year after we said "I do," MS threatened my health, our new marriage, and our active lifestyle.

The Breakdown

Doing it all wore me out, and the price I paid was my health. In trying to have it all, I forgot that I already did. I quickly understood how filling every moment of my day with stuff and busyness had made me sick.

There is no known cause or cure for multiple sclerosis, but I believe that MS was my body's way of rejecting my lifestyle. The way I was living didn't cause MS but it exacerbated my symptoms and contributed to relapses. My quest to do it all did not resonate with my heart. When you live or work outside of your heart, there will always be a breakup, a breakdown, or both. Working more, owning more, doing more, and trying to prove to everyone around me that I was more wore me down and literally broke my body.

I'll tell you about my diagnosis, but this book isn't about my MS. Instead it's about the changes and shifts that MS inspired. At first, I thought my disease would ruin everything, but instead, it saved me in every possible way. When I learned how damaging stress is for people with MS, other autoimmune conditions, and all people suffering from pain or sickness, I decided to eliminate as much of it as possible. I wanted to live well with MS, better than how I was living before my diagnosis. Once I intentionally began to slow down and simplify my life, I began to heal, and most of the healing had nothing to do with multiple sclerosis. Through the process of figuring out what my body needed and what my heart wanted, a soulful simplicity quietly emerged as a different way of being. It wasn't a spiritual awakening or one of those "woo-woo" moments. It was a gentle honesty about what mattered most in my life. When I started asking questions about what was important and identified what wasn't, I discovered what truly resonated with my heart and soul. I took the time to listen to myself. I learned to trust the answers, and I began to live simply and soulfully.

This wasn't the first time I had considered the possibility of living more simply. Years before, I had read *Your Money or Your Life* by Vicki Robin and Joe Dominguez and thought it was brilliant, but I gave up on the idea of living with less because I was in so much debt and overextended in most areas of my life. Actually, I gave up because it sounded too hard. Living the way I was living was difficult, but at least I knew how to do it. Simplicity author Elaine St. James said, "One of the reasons we keep our lives so complicated is so we won't have to listen to our inner voice telling us what we need to do to make our lives work better."

I leaned into simplicity, and when I say leaned, I mean I started slowly. I saw the potential in simplifying, but I didn't want to shake up my life. Extreme changes would only cause more stress. This soulful simplicity had to match not only my heart and soul but the heart and soul of my family. I had a tendency of trying to change everything all at once. This time was different. This time I made one change at a time, giving it as much time as it needed. Then I'd use the momentum and confidence I'd built from one change to start the next.

Gradually, I began to see how simplicity allowed hope to replace fear, and I became healthier and happier than I was before my diagnosis. Over time, my entire family embraced a simpler life and discovered the soulfulness within it. As a result, I felt better physically and emotionally and changed my life in ways I had never imagined. Today, my life looks completely different from how it did ten years ago, and it's so much better. While I have radically simplified my life, I did it very gently. Through the process, I discovered that it isn't about organizing things or just getting rid of stuff. Those are the mechanics and certainly part of it all, but simplicity is about more than making space in your home. It's also about creating more time in your life and more love in your heart. What I learned is that you can actually be more with less.

In 2010 I began to document my journey with a blog in hopes of connecting with like-minded people and to share what I was learning. I've shared the good, like my last yard sale ever and downsizing from 2,000 square feet to 750; the bad, like struggling to let go of items I held on to "just in case"; and even the ugly: when I displayed the inventory of my $2,500 cosmetic collection, wondering why I was living paycheck to paycheck. Sharing my life online is scary sometimes, but usually very rewarding. I've met the most thoughtful, compassionate people, created a career writing and speaking about the power of simplicity, and been forever changed by sharing my story.

I should mention that this is not the book I was supposed to write or the book some people told me I should write. It's the book I wanted and needed to write to make a difference for the right people—maybe for you. I believe the only way to make a difference is to connect heart to heart, so the only choice I had was to write down my heart on each page of this book for a chance to connect with yours. I wrote this book to share my soulful simplicity with you, and perhaps it will help you discover your own. If you've ever felt sick and tired of being broke, stressed, overworked, and never catching up, living more simply can bring more purpose and intention into your life. Headaches, anxiety, depression, or a general feeling of overwhelm are often a result of "excess" in our lives. You don't have to be diagnosed with MS or some other disease to benefit from a life that is scaled back and pared down. My MS diagnosis was my "enough is enough" moment. Yours might be different.

I made some very big changes in four areas of my life: health, space, time, and love. By choosing less, I reclaimed more of each. Every big change I made was the result of hundreds of small steps and stories. In the chapters that follow, I'll share those steps and stories. I'll tell you what brought me back to health and love, and I'll ask you to consider what might work for you. Start to think about what really matters to you. If you aren't sure at first, don't worry. Sometimes you have to get rid of the things that don't matter to let the things that do rise to the surface. At the end of each section, you'll find a soul-searching/heart-listening practice and a list of small steps to work into your soulful simplicity. As you simplify your life, you'll create the time and space you need to listen to your body, know your heart, and connect to your soul. There isn't a one-size-fits-all solution to simplifying your life, but I hope my story will inspire your journey of living with less . . . and then so much more.

MAKING ME: I HAD TO START WITH THE INSIDE

When You Live or Work Outside of Your Heart, There Will Always Be a Breakup, Breakdown, or Both

I forgot who I was. For a really long time, I forgot who I was. It looked like I knew from the outside. I even believed it myself most of the time, but by the way I was building and living my life, it's clear I had forgotten. There are times when I wonder if things would have been better if I hadn't made the mistakes I made, but I rarely go down that road. I'm confident that because I got lost, disconnected, and turned upside down, I was able to come out even better on the other side and experience the kind of gratitude you just can't tap into unless you know what it's like to live outside of your heart. Not being yourself is exhausting and breaks you down from the inside out. Simplifying my life was the way I remembered who I was. When we hear about the benefits of simplicity, we immediately think of organized sock drawers, clean countertops, and tidy bookshelves, but it's much more than that if you want it to be.

Remembering yourself, connecting with your heart, making you—these are all surprising results of getting simple. You used to know who you were, but all the stuff, obligations, and craziness of life got in the way and clouded your vision. Getting rid of everything that doesn't matter allows you to remember who you are. Simplicity doesn't change who you are, it brings you back to who you are. Simplifying your life invites you to start peeling back the layers of excess, outside and in. Once you remove all the things that have been covering you up and holding you back, you can step into yourself, back into your heart, and be you again.

My soulful simplicity started with making me, and once I had a glimpse of remembering who I was, what I stood for, and what made me smile, I wanted more. With each thing I let go of, I took another step closer to the real me. As I made more space, more time, and more love, I remembered me. Now many years later, I've become fiercely protective of the connection I have with my heart and soul. Just remembering wasn't enough. I have to continue to build on what I'm remembering and learning about myself. That consistent attention to who I am makes me more giving and loving and allows me to be perfectly content in almost any situation. I have to believe that contributes to my health and relationships in ways I may never fully understand.

The first section of this book starts with us: making me, and making you. I thought this was the best place to start because it's where everything starts.

CHAPTER ONE

An Ironic Diagnosis

I could feel the gadolinium contrast pushing through my vein. A wave of warmth rushed up my arm, and then through my entire body. I knew my face was flushed. Then, as they slid me back into the MRI machine, nausea hit, and then the panic. "There is no room to sit up. I am going to throw up and choke on my own vomit." My head was in a plastic cage snapped tightly shut, my arms were down by my side, and the machine started to shake and sounded like ten thousand jackhammers. I hadn't let myself get really scared until now. For months, I'd been fighting vertigo, fatigue, and other symptoms, chalking it all up to stress and an ear infection. I was training for the Harmon's MS 150, a cycling event in Salt Lake City, in the spring of 2006. I was going to our local recreation center for indoor training sessions because it was still too cold to ride outdoors.

I didn't know much about multiple sclerosis, but my boss had it. I worked for a publishing company and the owner was in a wheelchair. When I first started working for him, I didn't know what was wrong with him and I was too intimidated to ask. Even though he was in a wheelchair, he was a powerhouse. He was committed to his company and enjoyed the stressful nature of the business, and made it more stressful whenever he could. Eventually, I found John's softer side. I had great respect for him and his wife even though we couldn't be more different. That stress they thrived on twisted me up. Once I got to know them better and had been with the company for almost two years, I decided to raise money for MS research by participating in the 150-kilometer ride. I wasn't sure if I'd ride the whole thing but I was looking forward to trying. I wanted to raise money for MS research, but I was really riding for John, for his softer side.

It was a stressful spring, and there were several events that likely triggered the exacerbation that led to my diagnosis. I was working long hours and had volunteered to chair the annual auction at my daughter's school. I took a little detour from my cycling training and went to visit my sister, who lived in Germany. I was so excited to see her, my brother-in-law, and my niece and nephew. We didn't see each other very often because we were an ocean apart, but we talked almost every day or exchanged messages. We weren't always the best of friends when we were kids, but we get closer and closer year after year. Bailey, Mark, and I went together and we had a blast. Between afternoon prosecco toasts celebrating our reunion and late nights, though, I completely stressed out my already stressed-out body. Add work deadlines and jet lag, and it's no wonder that I didn't feel well when I got back. My grandfather died that spring too. Research shows stress can cause MS relapses or episodes. I was just getting by in the craziness of my life, just making ends meet, just barely handling it. On the outside, it looked like balance. On the inside, it felt like hell. Losing my grandfather tipped the scales.

• • •

When my grandfather died, he was living in an Alzheimer's facility. It was always hard to visit him because he always remembered me, but couldn't really remember why he was there, why he didn't have his driver's license, and why his life was gone, but he was still here. On the day he died, I spent most of the day with him. His eyes were closed and he was lying down, but he wasn't peaceful. He was agitated, frustrated, restless. Pissed, really. Not completely lucid, but feisty and verbal. Some things never change. He kept raising his arms up and saying "Lift me up, pull me up," over and over again. I'd lift him up and fluff his pillow and he'd start all over again. I could not make him comfortable. I've lost people before. Friends, my grandmother, other more distant relatives, but I've never been with them when they left. It wasn't the peaceful passing I had heard about. It was volatile and awful.

For months I had nightmares about my grandfather yelling at me, "Lift me up, pull me up!" Those words and moments haunted me. About six months after he died, I asked a minister at my church to meet me for coffee so I could tell her how mad I was that God let my grandfather die like that and I couldn't help him. I couldn't ease his pain. I repeated the words. I said, "He kept yelling at me and raising his arms: 'Lift me up. Pull me up.'" After a moment of quiet contemplation, she looked at me and said very matter-of-factly, "Maybe he wasn't talking to you."

I thought about each of those stressful moments as I lay in the MRI tube, choking down the bile rising in my throat, and pushing back tears and panic, I started to pray, or plead, or some messy combination of the two, trapped in the tiny tube. "Please don't let me die in this machine. Please don't let me have a brain tumor or some crazy disease. Get me out of here. Get me out of here." By "here," I meant the machine, the hospital, the day, and the nightmare. Get me out of here.

I was living in the perfect storm of stress in my life: lack of sleep, overworking, jet lag, regular life stress, and the loss of someone I had loved my whole life. The vertigo was joined by overwhelming fatigue, tingly hands, and a numbness in part of my face. I was sad, tired, and completely depleted and sick. I thought the vertigo was an ear infection and my doctor thought so too, at least that's what he told me. Two weeks later, I still couldn't walk a straight line, let alone ride a bike, and I went back to the doctor. We started with MRIs of the head. Lesions suggested something, but nothing definitive. More tests: ear testing, eye testing, spinal cord MRIs, heart ultrasounds. Was I having mini strokes? Did I have ALS? The last test, a spinal tap, sealed the deal.

That's when I got the phone call from my doctor at the neurology office. At first, she told me I didn't have MS, and we should take a "wait and see approach" to determine the next step. She said she was surprised no one had called me since they got the results the week before. I told her I had only had the test a few days ago. She said she had to call me back. Three minutes later, she called back and said, "Oops. I was looking at the wrong chart. Yep, you have MS."

This wasn't the defining moment, although it felt like it for a while. It was the scariest moment and the messiest. My fate was delivered over the phone, while I was at work, as casually as "Do you want fries with that?" I didn't know what to do with the information. I had no next step, no plan, only fear.

I had missed the MS ride, was diagnosed with MS while raising money for it, and still couldn't get on my bike. I hung up the phone, cried all the way home, and took a Valium left over from treating the ear infection I never had.

CHAPTER TWO

Let's Go for Ice Cream

One of the hardest things I had to do was tell my daughter I was sick. I had checked some library books out a few weeks earlier and read nearly everything I could about MS. Because I didn't know if I had it or not, I wasn't as interested in the treatments as the symptoms. What was going to happen to my body if I did have MS? Nothing good, according to these books. I could go blind or get double vision from optic neuritis, I might lose or struggle with bowel and bladder function, experience cognitive decline or end up in a wheelchair. These books were decades old, and conventional treatments had only been available for less than twenty years. They made MS sound like a death sentence—or worse—in my mind. I knew the first thing I had to do was tell everyone what was happening. It never crossed my mind to keep this a secret even though I knew it would be scary to talk about it. What would people think? Did they even know what MS was? The adults in my immediate family knew what was going on, but other family, friends, and coworkers had no idea.

The last person in the family I told was my daughter. It was the conversation I was dreading most. Bailey and I are close. She is my everything. I was divorced when she was three, after seven years of marriage, although I knew I'd be leaving from the day she was born. Raising a child for so many years alone provides a unique bond. Bailey and I are so alike. People tell us all the time that we even use the same facial expressions. I could never say in words how I feel about this child, and that's why telling her that I was sick was so hard. I peeked into her bedroom and said, "Let's go for ice cream." I took her to an ice-cream shop down the street from our house. For some reason, I thought a happy place would discount or offset the sad news. I also needed the leverage of an environment that would keep her from running to her room. I wanted space for emotion, for questions, for comfort. Most of all, I just wanted to soften the blow.

We sat down at the table with our cups of ice cream and I attempted to make small talk. And then I said, "Remember how I had vertigo and was going to the doctor?" Of course she did. And then I said something ridiculous like "Don't be scared" or "This isn't as bad as it sounds," and before I said another word, tears pooled in her eyes, her beautiful brown eyes. And I said, "I have MS." She started crying and said, "I knew it." She left her ice cream and ran out the door. I followed her, unlocked the car, and we both got in the backseat. I felt like I was stealing her childhood and wanted to cry. Not for me or the MS, but because I couldn't possibly know what was going on in that little heart and brain. I knew she was strong enough to go through this with me, but my instinct to protect her was strong too. I understood why so many parents hide the pain they are experiencing from their children. I quickly told her the two things I thought she needed to hear, and that I fiercely believed in that moment: "I'm not going to die" and

"You aren't going to get it." We cried and cuddled in the backseat for a while and when she calmed down enough, I brought her home and we relocated to her bedroom. We jumped in her bed, cuddled up, and talked quietly. She told me that she had seen the library books about MS in the car a few weeks ago. I told her I didn't know then, that it was only a possibility. Had I known she was already worried, I would have started the conversation sooner. See, kids are smart. They see and hear things. If you've ever tried to hide something from your children, you know what I mean. If we don't step in and share with them and include them, they imagine things much worse than reality. I told her that while things felt really scary right now, that was going to change. I told her that MS wasn't going to be the center of our lives and that after a few months, it would become the new normal. As we both calmed down and kept talking, my uncertainty began to melt. In that moment, I went from scared and worried to knowing that I would fight for my health and win. I would do that for us.

We fell asleep, and when we woke up we were a little less scared than the night before.

CHAPTER THREE

Love and Other Drugs

Let's start with the love part. Love was more powerful than any conventional therapy I tried. It still is. In the beginning, love was . . . the calls with my sister when I didn't know what was wrong with me. She was across the ocean but it felt like she was holding my hand. Love was the way my husband found a thousand ways to help me before I even knew how to ask for help. Love was how my parents rallied around me and said they would do anything to help. Love was the time my daughter got in trouble for writing about the benefits of stem cell therapy for MS at her Catholic school, and love was when my sister-in-law organized a cycling team, Team TLC (the team who loves Courtney), to raise funds for MS research. All of those loving things, along with many others, healed me.

For the Love of Puppy Breath

Three weeks after my MS diagnosis, we happened to be watching a local pet adoption cable channel, and our hearts broke over every sad pet story. We weren't considering a puppy, even though Bailey had wanted one, so I'm not exactly sure how we got hooked on that channel. Then a dog named Lloyd was featured. Lloyd was a little black puppy with brain damage. I thought about my recent MRI scans. I had brain damage too. "We're meant for each other," I thought. Before I knew it, my heart (or my brain damage) took over and I said, "We're adopting Lloyd." I was usually the voice of reason in the family—or at least willing to discuss big decisions before jumping—but I had made up my mind. My husband was speechless, and my daughter hugged me.

I was over the moon. I thought I wanted to heal Lloyd, but what I really wanted was for Lloyd to heal me and to heal our family. We needed some good news, something to lift our spirits after weeks of scary health stuff. Lloyd seemed like the perfect lift. After talking with Lloyd's foster mom, though, we learned that his needs were far outside our capabilities. Lloyd needed a stay-at-home parent, and I wasn't that. I was a busy, working mom with a chronic disease. I didn't have the time that Lloyd deserved. It was heartbreaking to realize Lloyd wouldn't become part of our family, but once I had said "yes" to one puppy, we couldn't close the door. We decided to look at other puppies. Clearly, my desire for simplicity hadn't kicked in yet. I just wanted some relief from the pain and heaviness. I wanted to be light.

We drove to a local animal shelter, where there was a litter of shepherd-ish mutts. Bailey and I walked to an outdoor pen and were immediately surrounded by little whimpering black and tan puppies. One pup immediately jumped up and gave Bailey a big hug. When she knelt down, he actually threw his front paws around her neck. That's how she knew he was ours. We didn't care about his manners, breeding, or anything else. We named our new little ray of light Guinness.

Guinness was an energetic puppy, and when I say energetic, I mean he was always running around, puppy nose in everything, and constantly underfoot. Mark told me not to worry. He said, "He'll settle down in a couple of years." Mark told me that "settling down story" every year for eight years. Even when Guinness was crazy with puppy energy, though, he knew when I needed him to be on extra good behavior. When I was recovering from an MS treatment or feeling down, he cuddled up quietly next to me. When I changed treatments a year after my diagnosis, I'd nap and recover for a full day or two after my monthly infusion, and Guinness would lie down in bed with me most of the day. He healed me as much as any treatments or other changes I made in my life. There is encouraging research available on the healing power of dogs. Petting a dog can release oxytocin, serotonin, and prolactin in the brain, improving mood and reducing physical pain. It also lowers cortisol, a chemical associated with stress. If petting does all that, I can only imagine the healing I experienced after our daylong cuddle sessions. I didn't know the research then, but my heart knew something was happening on a cellular level each time I made eye contact with my boy, or rubbed his puppy belly.

Other Drugs

Researching and learning about MS became my new full-time job, on top of my full-time job. Before picking a drug therapy, I researched the four that were available at the time. My shitty doctor, the one who confused my chart and diagnosed me over the phone, suggested I stop by and review a few pharmaceutical marketing kits and pick a drug. I was supposed to pick my own drug? I had no idea what I was doing, but logically, I wanted the strongest, most powerful therapy available, which to me meant the highest dose, delivered the most frequently. Sounds reasonable, right? Not the pick-your-own-drug part, but equating more with better? I spent an afternoon learning to inject needles into oranges. I had done my best to keep it all together, but when a home nurse was explaining things and teaching me how to pierce my own skin with a needle, my body seemed to float up. I was looking down at my kitchen table covered with oranges and syringes and I just thought, "Is this my life now?" and I cried.

Soon I was injecting interferons into my body three times a week with no tears. I used auto injectors, so I didn't have to actually stick the needle in, and they violently shot the meds into the fat on my belly, arms, and legs. It was one of the few times I've been glad to have a little extra. According to the label, the most common side effect of the injection was "flu-like symptoms," but to me, they were "malaria-like symptoms." I'd go to work sweating, pasty, and shaking. I was taking medicine to calm the nausea, and I lost myself in the haze of the side effects. I didn't think anyone noticed, though, so I kept going. I just kept going.

While I was trying to get used to my new normal and injecting what felt like poison into my body, I was researching other alternatives too. I attended an MS support group and asked the medical professional if a very expensive nutritional supplement I had read about online could be the answer. Because the Internet has a cure for everything. A pharmaceutical rep sitting in the back jumped in and answered my question with a question: "What do you believe?" *Making me* started there. His question reminded me that I had a voice and that I knew my body better than any doctor I'd seen or article I had read. I had more to offer myself.

I introduced myself to him after the session ended and found out that this very successful pharmaceutical rep was a competitive cyclist and in great health, and he had MS too. The next day we were having lunch with our spouses. I wanted to know how he did it, how things were for his wife, what meds he took, what he ate. We talked for hours and on top of sharing his life experience, he brought pages and pages of clinical trials, studies, and other research. I didn't understand most of it, but I was willing to figure it out. I flunked basic math, science, and pretty much my whole first year of college, but this had my attention. His question, "What do you believe?" was more powerful than I thought. Once I knew what I believed or that what I believed mattered, my heart and soul were on board. All I needed to successfully fight this disease was to spend time with someone who already did. That lunch meeting gave me even more confidence to fight for my life: my life, my lifestyle, my happiness, and love. Now my heart was in the game. Instead of other people telling me how to treat my body, I was going to decide. I fired my neurologist and hired someone who was willing to make decisions with me and let me be my own advocate. It was time to take responsibility for the fact that I had some control here. I didn't choose MS, but I did choose what I put in my body, what medicine I took, what I ate, what I thought. I wasn't a victim or an innocent bystander. I quickly realized that while I wasn't responsible for my MS, I was responsible to it.

After almost a year of suffering through injections that made me feel worse than MS, I started the conversation about switching drugs with my family and my doctor. Everyone's initial reaction was no, but I knew it was fear talking. They were afraid of side effects that could be deadly. I had fear too but my fear was different. I was less afraid of the side effects and more afraid I was missing my life. The interferons made my body ache and my brain fuzzy. I could barely help my daughter through her fourth-grade homework. I was too tired to make it to the gym, and when you feel like crap for long enough, you start treating yourself and everyone around you like crap. I felt like I was on a steady decline, and this new drug with the risky side effects had the potential to turn things around.

There were times during that transition when I thought about going off conventional therapy altogether. Why couldn't I just be really healthy and fight MS? It was a possibility, but risky too. When I was finally given the okay from my neurologist to switch therapies, I had to take a month to "wash out" the drug in my system. At the end of that month, I remember one evening when my husband came home from work. I was cooking dinner. I was actually cooking dinner. I smiled as he walked into the kitchen. I was happy to see him. Before I said a thing, he said, "Wow, it's nice to have you back."

I knew I couldn't fight this disease with love and drugs alone, and started to research other complementary treatments. I went with my gut mostly in deciding what to try: Yoga: yes. Craniosacral massage: sure. Bee stings: um, no thanks. I started to trust myself, remember myself.

Let's Get Back to Love

I'm not interested in debating the pros and cons of conventional medicine. Making a choice like that is deeply personal and I'd never suggest that taking or not taking pharmaceutical drugs is right for anyone. It has been the right choice for me. I have shrinking lesions and nine years of no MS progression or relapses to prove that, but I do not believe the drugs can stand alone. This goes for almost anything you suffer from. Without love for yourself, and love for how you live, and who you spend your time with, the drugs aren't going to be helpful for very long, if ever. And saying or thinking you love yourself is not enough either. Love is reflected in your daily choices. When you choose crappy food for lunch, that isn't loving. Neither is choosing work over sleep or anger over gratitude. They are all choices. Not easy ones, but choices nonetheless. I wish I could say that I make loving choices all the time, but I don't. More than I used to, but I'm not even a little bit close to perfect. That said, now that I acknowledge that they are my choices, and they are directly connected with how I feel about myself and my life, it's easier to lean toward love.

MS was my immediate pain point and wake-up call, but had I really been paying attention, I would have been woken up sooner. Take a look at your pain points, your suffering. It may be a chronic condition or disease, something easy to identify, or maybe it's something else like a strained relationship, the stress of overdue bills, general fatigue, or just a sense of "something isn't right." Those things may feel normal like they did for me, but you deserve better. Use any of them or all of them as a catalyst for change.

I realized I needed more time and space to put my health first, more time and space to listen to my heart and connect with my soul. I needed more room for rest, more room for research, and just more room for room.

CHAPTER FOUR

Making You

I'm going to tell you more about making me, but first I want to check in with you. This first section is mostly about me: how I got to a place where things fell apart, and why I decided to put the pieces together in a completely new way. The next three sections dig into more stories and practical steps to help you simplify your life, and suggestions on how to make or remake your space, your time, and most important, your love. I'll continue to share my experiences too, but as much as this book is about me, it is about you.

While you are reading, think about your wake-up calls, your breakups, your breakdowns, and the times you've had the opportunity to put the pieces back together. Look for the common threads—not just the bad threads, but the good ones too. I often find my story in other people's stories. We are much more alike than we think. That's the power of sharing the things that happen to us and how we experience them. Perhaps your breakdown wasn't a scary diagnosis, and your breakup had nothing to do with a marriage . . . or maybe it did. The actual wake-up call is not nearly as important as what happens next, and the opportunity to respond to it has no time limit. If your wake-up call came years ago, this is the perfect time to take action and turn it into something powerful. You have an opportunity to rewrite your story and change things about your life, or your whole life. If guilt or regret has gotten in the way of change, let it go. Use your feelings of guilt, frustration, and discomfort to motivate a change. Make a change to encourage more health, peace, and love in your life. Make a change and do what is best for you.

It's been more than a decade since I answered my wake-up call and began to radically, but very slowly, change my life. I changed my diet, paid off my debt, decluttered my home until there were empty rooms, cleaned out my closet, quit my job, created work I love, downsized from a big house to a small apartment, deepened my relationships, owned my introvertedness, became soul-centered, and took my life back.

I didn't plan to make all of these changes, but each one inspired and encouraged the next. Ten years might sound like a long time to change, but it feels like the blink of an eye. A scary diagnosis was my invitation to change. I had other wake-up calls, but I was too busy and distracted to hear, let alone answer them. Once I made a little time and space to hear my inner voice, to really listen, changing got easier, even exciting. As my inner voice became easier to hear, I was able to connect with my heart and gain more clarity about what I really wanted in my life.

Maybe This Is Your Wake-up Call

My wake-up call was a phone call from my neurologist's office telling me I had multiple sclerosis. I didn't need someone to tell me I was sick to know I was. I knew things weren't right, but it felt easier to just keep going.

How many times have you thought "this isn't working" or "something's not right" or "things have to change"?—those thoughts and words are from your inner voice. It's your wake-up call calling. You don't need a scary diagnosis or major crisis to wake up. No one needs to tell you because you already know. Your inner voice has been trying to tell you, but in case it's been a challenge to find time and space to listen through the chaos, see if you can find your wake-up call here.

THIS IS YOUR WAKE-UP CALL . . .

- If your life is on autopilot.
- If you never put yourself first.
- If you've become someone you don't recognize to please other people or to chase some version of success that doesn't resonate with you.
- If you are constantly self-medicating with food, shopping, booze, TV, or other distractions.
- If you are worn down, beat up, stressed out, and completely depleted.

Getting your wake-up call is not the hard part, even though it might hurt a little bit. Answering the call is. Choosing to answer the call instead of ignoring it is hard because you know if you do, things are going to change, and change is scary. That said, ignoring your call is worse, especially once you know it's time to change.

So often we want to jump into action. We want the road map or step-by-step instructions, but part of making you is making the map. Before you begin to create the map it helps to have a clear understanding of why you need a map in the first place. Why simplicity? Why change? What is motivating your journey? The answers will be different for everyone and they may change over time, but having a strong list of whys will encourage you along the way, especially if things get tough. Simplicity and most big change are a matter of the heart. If your heart isn't in the game, permanent change doesn't stand a chance. Really understand your motivation to change. What's pulling on your heart? For instance, quitting sugar to lose ten pounds to fit into your high school jeans for a reunion may get your ego's attention, but it might not speak to your heart; but if you think quitting sugar will help you sleep better, prevent cancer, and live longer . . . now it's a matter of the heart. Change is scary, but looking back over the past ten years, I'm so grateful I did it despite my fear. The more stress I released, the more time and space I created. Finally, there was room for more love: self-love, love for my family, work I love . . . all the love. Each change I made to simplify my life demonstrated that less stuff = more love.

I can't tell you what your reasons are, but I do know once you identify them, vocalize them, and write them down, you will never look back. Once simplifying your life becomes a matter of the heart, you will connect with like-minded people and find the strength you need to let go of the clutter, the busyness, and all of the other things standing between you and what matters most. One thing to note about living a soulful simplicity is that it's not a quick fix or something you do once. It's more like exercise where you have to keep practicing, keep starting over, and keep coming back. It's always here for you, but it's up to you to practice, connect, and reconnect with it.

Make this journey about making you. Think about what you are made of, and what you want your life to be. Then make it.

CHAPTER FIVE

Lessons from the Mat

The first time someone suggested I take a yoga class, I was insulted. I thought they were trying to find a slow, easy sport for me and my MS. There I was doing everything I could to be healthy with MS and they were giving up on me. I wanted to play tennis, go to the gym, and climb mountains and they wanted me to stretch.

If you've ever been to a yoga class, you know I had no idea what I was talking about. A few months later, I walked into my first yoga class and never stopped. Yoga changed me inside and out and it wasn't easy or slow. Within a week or two of my first class, I started taking private sessions at five a.m. a few times a week. I wanted to develop a practice I could take anywhere. That decision has served me again and again over the years. When yoga studios close, my favorite teachers move on, or I'm traveling or don't get to the studio for a while, I can always unroll my mat and practice. Even after many years of practice, I don't do handstands or some of the more challenging poses, but I move my body, put my hands on my heart, and listen for the lessons, the answers, and the truth. Yoga has been a big part of making me and continues to teach me new things about myself and the world. Here are just a few of my lessons from the mat. They've informed my work, my relationships, and how I move through every day.

1. My thoughts limit my actions.

When a challenging pose is being demonstrated, my go-to reaction is "not in this lifetime." And with that, my brain takes over and reminds my body that my hamstrings are too tight or my arms are too short or the pose will hurt my knees/shoulders/insert other body parts here. We dismiss opportunities every day by telling ourselves we can't do it. We give in to fear. It's good to think things through, but trust yourself to try new things too. If I never tried things I didn't think I could do, I never would have started a blog, written this book, or hiked across the jagged ridgeline of Cardiac Ridge in the Wasatch Mountains.

2. I can't do everything today.

Some days on the mat are a breeze. My mind is naturally quiet and my body flows effortlessly from pose to pose. Other times, I am so wrapped up in my own thoughts that it's a struggle just to relax my jaw. I used to feel defeated going into class with a busy mind, low energy, or a tweaked knee because I wouldn't be able to do every pose. Then I learned that it is okay to do what I can today. Much like a yoga class, our days are full of options and opportunity. We don't have to do it all. We can't do it all. We are better for it when we don't try to do it all.

3. **We all need permission to exhale.**

Heavy sighs often represent exhaustion or dissatisfaction, but several times throughout a yoga class, the teacher invites us to take a deep breath in through the nose and to let it all out with a big sigh. It feels so good to let it all go. In class, we might be releasing energy from a high-paced sequence and helping the heart rate come down, but think of the benefits a big exhale can have in your day-to-day life. In *Learning to Breathe*, author Priscilla Warner says SIGH stands for Sitting In God's Hands. There you go . . . permission to sigh, to take a seat in God's hands. Take a deep breath in through your nose and then release it through your mouth with a big sigh the next time you are in traffic, running late, frustrated, excited, stressed, or anxious.

4. **There is a place between ease and strain.**

When I practice balance poses, I weave and wobble if there isn't enough tension in my body. Likewise, if my jaw is clenched, eyebrows furrowed, and gaze locked, I can't find stillness and I fall out of the pose. If I push or back off just a tiny bit, I find that magical place between ease and strain called steadiness. Hard work isn't always a sign of good work. Steadiness can improve relationships, foster creativity, and improve health.

5. **Action kills fear.**

In certain yoga poses, I am afraid that I will literally fall right on my face and break my nose. It's very unlikely, but the fear is there. When I am creating something or putting myself out there in life, I am equally afraid of falling on my face and breaking my heart.

I have fallen in both yoga and life, but my nose is relatively straight and my heart is strong. Fear is okay and action will always shut it down.

6. **Keep your eyes on your own mat.**

My yoga pose doesn't have to look like yours to be magnificent. Each pose is an individual expression that represents our abilities, emotions, what we had for breakfast, and so many other things. There is no benefit in comparison in yoga or in life.

7. **Outward actions are directly connected to internal reactions.**

The final pose of a yoga class is called Savasana or corpse pose. It's the place where you release everything. You stop controlling your breath and holding your body in poses that may be challenging. You are finally invited to completely let go. It is there I learned that letting go is the hardest pose of all, and not just on the yoga mat. We work so hard to make everyone happy, stay caught up, be everywhere, appear like we have it all figured out, and do it all with a smile. Even when we are doing things we love, we sometimes push too much or hold on too tight. It's as if we think that with sheer will, we can bend the universe and magically design a desirable outcome.

Do a quick check right now. Is your jaw clenched? Are your toes curled? Are you holding your breath? Those are the tiny physical signs of the bigger mental and emotional attempt to control the world, or at least your world. There will be times when you think that you are there. You'll think you've completely let go, only to discover a tight grip on your grocery cart when you see the price of spinach or a long line at the registers. One day, in my final yoga pose of class, when I was seemingly completely relaxed and unattached, my yoga teacher said, "Come on people, let the monkey off the chain," and I did. I let go of intensity and control and focus. I melted into the mat . . . and smiled.

When it comes to letting go, you don't need an elaborate how-to list or instruction manual. Just release your jaw, soften your gaze, breathe . . . and smile. When you notice yourself pulling, prodding, forcing, resisting, and holding on for dear life, let the monkey off the chain.

CHAPTER SIX

Do Things You Don't Want to Do

I write about and sing the praises of living a healthy lifestyle, simplifying life, and doing work that matters, but I think it's important to note that I don't always want to do the things I do. For example, I drink smoothies full of greens most mornings. I've been doing that for a long time. Leafy greens fuel me. They make me feel good, and I have come to really enjoy them. That said, sometimes I want to eat waffles, and bacon, and drink a Bloody Mary instead. I don't, but I want to.

Before breakfast, one of the last things I want to do is exercise. Even though I'm happy once I start moving, those moments between my 5:30 wake-up and stepping into the gym aren't all rainbows and dreamy thoughts about how excited I am to sweat. I didn't want to clean out my clutter either or spend years paying off debt, but I did want to be clutter-free and debt-free. Over almost a decade of massive change, it's become very clear to me that you have to do things you don't want to do so you can do things you want to do and have the kind of life you really want.

With the exception of adrenaline junkies who like to jump off cliffs and run ultramarathons, most of us enjoy the path of least resistance. We want all of the benefits and less of the work. I believe that we should intentionally choose how we spend our time and engage in activities that bring real joy to our lives, so it may seem like a mixed message that I think we have to do things that we don't want to do to get there. Luckily, with the exception of paying taxes and routine dental cleanings, I find the joy once I get started doing things I don't want to do. I do things I don't want to do so I can be healthy. I do them so I can feel energized and be creative. I do things I don't like because I am curious and because I like being open to things that scare me (but not spiders). And really, because all the things I think I don't want to do usually offer an enjoyable twist or important lesson or benefit. The first few minutes before my blender starts in the morning, just before the coconut water turns green from pureed spinach and kale, I sometimes want to jump back in bed, order pizza, and watch sappy Drew Barrymore movies, but I know where that goes and make a choice to go another way. I still enjoy pizza and watching movies all day (my favorite is *Fever Pitch*), but not on a regular basis.

If I had to identify the three things I do that have the biggest impact on my health, they'd be:

1. **Eating greens and other real food.** When I was diagnosed with MS, I got very serious about changing my diet. All of the research I did pointed to eliminating animal protein. I experimented with raw and vegan diets and was a vegetarian for many years after my diagnosis. I recently added some fish and seafood to my diet and dropped most of the bread and pasta I was consuming

and I focus on eating more real food. Because how our bodies react to food varies so much, it's important to experiment on your own to see what works best for you, and to be open to the idea that what's best may change over time. I highly recommend trying the Whole30 to learn more about what is best for your body. It's a challenge that founders Melissa and Dallas Hartwig describe as "a short-term nutritional reset, designed to help you put an end to unhealthy cravings and habits, restore a healthy metabolism, heal your digestive tract, and balance your immune system." For thirty days, you eliminate sugar, grains, alcohol, dairy, and legumes. I've taken the Whole30 challenge several times, and I learn more about what my body really needs to thrive each time.

2. **Walking.** Walking isn't good only for my body, but for my mind, heart, and soul too. I leave my goals behind when I walk and notice my surroundings. Sometimes it's hard to break away from work during the day to take a walk, but each time I do, I return with more clarity and energy.

3. **Sleeping.** I aim for seven to eight hours of sleep every night. When I can't fall asleep, or I wake up and have trouble falling back asleep, I meditate myself back to sleep with the Headspace app. Arianna Huffington, sleep crusader and author of *The Sleep Revolution,* says, "Our cultural assumption that overwork and burnout are the price we must pay in order to succeed is at the heart of our sleep crisis," and suggests that while rituals and other things can

help us sleep better, ultimately it starts with a mind-set shift. "To be able to leave the outside world behind each night when we go to sleep, we need to first recognize that we are more than our struggles and more than our victories and failures. We are not defined by our jobs and titles, and we are vastly more than our resumes. By helping us keep the world in perspective, sleep gives us a chance to refocus on the essence of who we are."

This doing things you don't want to do goes for work too. I love my work, really love it, but even with all of that love, there are parts of my job that I don't want to do. I don't want to do accounting or administrative stuff or deal with certain other parts of my work. Even when it comes to writing, there are little bits and pieces that I try to avoid. I didn't want to write a book proposal for this book, but I wanted to write the book so I wrote the proposal.

Even though I mostly do things that are right for my body, I slip and slide, eat junky food, and skip a workout or stay up late every now and then, but I pay the price, short-term and long. The nice thing is that the more consistent I am in practicing my healthy habits, the easier it is to come back to them when I do slide. What I want more than anything is to feel good enough to fully engage in the best parts of life. I didn't used to be as intentional about these things as I am now, and I honestly thought I was too busy to choose. When you live in a reactive state, making healthy choices can seem impossible. You can almost convince yourself that busyness and chaos aren't a choice, that you didn't create it. I used to eat and work in my car in between sales calls. It's much easier to eat something from a fast-food restaurant than to make a healthy salad at home. Waking up earlier to work out or finding time to create a new career felt completely out of reach before I simplified my life. So what do you do when you are too busy to choose? You still choose, because not choosing is a choice. There is another way. You can try again. As Thomas Edison said, "When you have exhausted all possibilities, remember this—you haven't." Interestingly enough, good choices encourage more good choices. When I work out, I feel more motivated to eat well, and vice versa.

I wasn't born a kale lover. I'm not naturally inclined to exercise and I had no idea how to run a business or start a blog. The reason I'm able to eat mostly fruits and vegetables, stay active, and grow in my work is not about motivation, determination, skill, or luck. It's because I do things that I don't want to do. I do things that make me uncomfortable, things that I don't think I'm capable of doing, and things I don't know how to do. I wish some of the books I've read or health and business coaches would talk more about that. We have to do things we don't want to do to be who we want to be and feel how we want to feel. And once we push through that tiny bit (or really big chunk) of resistance, we usually find we are doing exactly what we want. I was stuck until I was willing to get uncomfortable. If you want to get out of your slump or if you feel stuck, try something you've never done before or something that you really don't want to do. You don't have to be inspired or motivated. Just start. You can start right now. Make a list of ten things you don't want to do that you know will help you. You can probably list a hundred things, but start with ten. Choose one thing from your list that you really don't want to do and put it into action immediately. Don't wait or put it on your to-do list. Start small. Consistency will be more important than intensity. Here's an example: Let's say you want to eat more greens even though you don't want to eat more greens. Instead of trying to eat a big kale salad every day, commit to a forkful of greens at every meal. After a week, make it two forkfuls and so on.

Sometimes you have to do things you don't want to do so you can do the things you want to do.

CHAPTER SEVEN

Fewer Ends

I applied for my first credit card on a college campus before I ever set foot in a classroom. Within a year, I had two credit cards with the same company and was using one to pay the other. I probably don't need to clarify, but this was not a wise financial strategy. You'll be relieved to know I wasn't an accounting or math major. I went into debt fast and furiously and not out of necessity, but because I wanted more freedom and I thought that came in the form of money, even if I didn't have it to spend.

By the time I was looking for "a real job" in my early twenties, money was the number-one consideration. I had to make ends meet. Considering what I really wanted to do and how I wanted to spend my time never crossed my mind. Life became simply about making ends meet. I was constantly making decisions about what bills to pay, what to buy, and what to sacrifice. My twenties were about shuffling dollars around, making minimum payments, and asking collectors to back off. As stressful as that was, I tried to have a laissez-faire attitude about it all. I figured if my credit score was in the toilet, and I was already in debt for life, what's a little more? I faked out the people around me and even faked out my own heart from time to time. I was doing okay. I was making ends meet. Sort of.

There were quiet moments when I had pangs of guilt and uneasiness. This wasn't how I wanted to live. But instead of indulging in those moments, and giving them space to change me, I filled them up. I filled them with sweet treats, with shopping, a glass of wine or two or four, a vacation. I kept filling up the space and kept making ends meet.

I had never been an adult without owing someone money. As we were paring down our stuff and eliminating stress, Mark and I decided we weren't going to live in debt anymore. I called and canceled all my credit cards in one afternoon. MasterCard, The Gap, Victoria's Secret, JCPenney, Macy's . . . I called store after store, canceled the cards, and then cut them up. I was cutting up all the ends I worked so hard to meet year after year. Once those ends were gone, I began to look at the other ends in my life. The ends weren't just about money. Making ends meet impacted my entire life—keeping people happy, paying the bills, errands, meetings, obligations, commitments, getting things done, catching up—so many ends. Why was I always struggling to make them meet and trying to tie them up in a nice little bow? My attempts to stretch and meet and tie always ended in some sort of unraveling.

I finally figured it out. Instead of working so hard to make ends meet, work on having fewer ends.

CHAPTER EIGHT

Put Your Hands on Your Heart

My soulful simplicity was unfolding on the inside as I changed my diet, and on the outside as I was decluttering and working on fewer ends. The time and space I created on the outside gave me the clarity to refine the work I was doing on the inside. I'll tell you more about how I created that space and time in the next section, but one of the most important things I did was begin to listen to my heart in a very literal way. After writing quietly, or meditating—doing something to create a little stillness around me and in me—I put one hand on my heart and then cover it with the other hand, as if I were holding my heart. It's a gesture to tell my heart, "I've got you. I trust you. I am here to listen to you." And then I sit with my eyes softly looking down, or closed, and I wait. Sometimes there's nothing, just me sitting quietly holding my heart. But the more I practice, and the safer my heart feels, the more she speaks to me. This practice helped me develop the confidence to trust the voice inside that I'd been ignoring for so long. It continues to be an important practice for me, for being soul-centered and in living a soulful simplicity.

I discovered that my heart and soul have something to offer, and giving that connection room to guide me was making me—making me stronger, making me lighter, and making me . . . me.

The Woo

I mentioned in the introduction that discovering my soulful simplicity wasn't a "woo-woo" moment, and for the most part, I'm not very woo-woo myself. I'm not anti-woo and I stay open to considering that which doesn't have a bunch of logic or science to back it up. To put my level of woo into perspective, I love yoga and meditation and believe in things I can't see. I know miracles are possible but I don't consult tarot cards or feng shui my home. I'm not opposed to those things and think they may work very well for some, but they are not part of who I am. For those of you who do lean toward the woo, feel free to skim through this paragraph and get on with your heart practice. Your openness will serve you well as you put your hands on your heart. For those of you who are more like me, or even if you are skeptical or completely reject the woo, you might be thinking, "I can't believe she wants me to light a candle and hold my heart in my hands." I understand your resistance, but know that I don't consider this a mystical practice. I believe it's our right and responsibility to remember who we are and to show up in the world as that person. Remembering, loving, connecting, and knowing the how, what, why—it all starts here with your hands on your heart.

Put Your Hands on Your Heart

I'd like to invite you to join me and develop your own hands-on-heart practice. At the end of each section in the book, I'll ask you to sit quietly and begin to tap into your own soulful simplicity. Engage a little bit each day as you are reading this book and begin to establish your heart practice. If you're ready we can start now, or come back when you are.

Choose a time each day when you can sit alone quietly for a few minutes. While you don't need to do anything special, it may help to light a candle and keep a pen and paper nearby to jot down anything that comes up. Sit on the floor, a chair, your bed, anywhere you feel comfortable, and take a few breaths to settle in and recognize the significance of creating space to listen to your heart.

Try practicing in silence, or with soft music. After a few cleansing breaths in through the nose and out through the mouth, close your eyes, or turn your gaze down and continue focusing on your breath.

Next, place one hand on your heart, and cover your hand with the other. Feel your heart beating. Feel the warmth of your heart and your hands. Now, while continuing to breathe in and out with some intention, and while feeling the warmth, start a conversation with your heart.

SUGGESTED QUESTIONS ABOUT MAKING YOU:

How are things going in my life? Consider how you spent the last week, the last month, and the last year. Resist your default polite answer. Other people aren't asking, "How are you?" You are asking you.

How do I feel physically? Does your back feel strong or sore? How about your hips, or your knees? Are you in pain or do you feel well? This isn't a time for judgment, only noticing.

How do I feel emotionally? Go a little deeper. How do you feel on the inside?

What do I love about my life? What makes you smile as soon as you think about it? Whose faces fill your heart when you close your eyes?

Whom do I envy and what do I lie about? Author Gretchen Rubin suggests that the answers to these questions might reveal things you need to change in your life. She says envy shows you when somebody has something you wish you had, and when you lie about something you are showing yourself there is something that is not right in your life.

What changes do I want to make? What would you like to add to or subtract from your life? What new habits pique your attention?

What changes do I have to make? What are the changes you have to make to save a relationship, become healthy, or get your life back? The have-tos may be harder to admit than the want-tos.

Use these questions as a conversation starter. Ask other questions that come up, and be open to the answers. Be open and curious, and compassionate with yourself, as you develop this practice and new relationship with your heart. It might feel weird or uncomfortable to ask the questions. There might not be answers right away. Keep practicing. Listen and trust your heart. She knows things.

MAKING YOU: ACTION STEPS

Work through this list in any order, trying one thing at a time. This isn't a to-do list or a competition. Consider each action as an invitation to learn more about yourself, and to begin making you.

Figure out what you believe. Until someone asked me "What do you believe?" I forgot how much that mattered. Take some time to explore what you believe, not what you were taught to believe, or what you are supposed to believe, but what you believe when you are alone with your hands on your heart.

Identify your wake-up calls. Look back without regret at your breakups and breakdowns, and recognize the quieter calls too. How did you react? What is your pattern of dealing with your wake-up calls? Do you take action? Ignore them completely? Try to change but fall back into old habits? Notice the calls and how you respond. No judgment, only noticing.

Write down your why. What's pulling on your heart? A soulful simplicity is not an overnight transformation. These changes may take years, so your heart has to be in it. Why do you want to make changes? Why do you want things to be simpler? Write down all your whys and keep them front and center as a constant reminder and reinforcement.

Try a yoga class. Visit a local yoga studio and take a class. This goes for beginners and more advanced yoga students as well. Pay attention to the lessons you can take into your day-to-day life. What happens on the mat is only a tiny part of yoga.

SIGH—sit in God's hands. You can do this anytime, wherever you are. Do it when you wake up, in traffic, when you are frustrated, or even when you are feeling especially grateful. Take a deep breath in through your nose, and let it all out through your mouth. Make it big, deep, noisy, and meaningful. Repeat.

Find a little steadiness. Back off or go a little deeper to find that magical place between ease and strain. Things flow more freely here.

Notice when you compare. Here's why comparing doesn't work. We are usually comparing our beginnings with their endings, or our insides with their outsides. This isn't fair comparing. If you measure yourself, your life, or your work based on comparison, consider who you are and what you have to offer without measuring against others. Ask your heart how comparing has served you. If it hasn't, let it go.

Let the monkey off the chain. Uncurl your toes. Unclench your jaw. Loosen your grip. Stop trying to control anything and everything. If you don't think you can let go, sigh, and try again later.

Eat greens. Add something green to your plate at every meal. Steam spinach, toss a salad, or make a green smoothie. At first, it might feel weird to eat greens for breakfast, but once you begin to notice how they fuel you and ground you, you'll look forward to your morning greens.

Prioritize sleep. Redesign your bedroom and schedule to support seven to nine hours of sleep. Keep your sleeping space cool and dark, and free of TV, digital devices, and work distractions.

Take a walk. Move every day, preferably outdoors.

Do something you don't want to do so you can do the things you want to do. These things are usually things you've considered before but have either procrastinated or written off completely. Go back. Try them.

Consider fewer ends. Reframe your approach to making ends meet. Even though that's what you thought you were supposed to do, now you know there is a better way: fewer ends.

Listen to your heart. Take three minutes, five minutes, ten minutes, or as many minutes as you can devote each day and put your hands on your heart. This may be your first step in finally putting yourself first. Putting your hands on your heart isn't a mystical practice. It's your right and responsibility to remember who you are. If you will listen, your heart will help.

MAKING SPACE: CLEARING THE DEBT AND CLUTTER

If You Want to Get Clear on What Matters,
Get Rid of Everything That Doesn't

After I began making me, I wanted to clear more space for my healing and heart work. I didn't consider myself a hoarder, or a shopaholic, yet I had a two-thousand-square-foot home, a garage, and a backyard storage shed filled with stuff. Some stuff hadn't been out of boxes in years. I didn't even really know what I had. All of our closets were filled, and of course, each of the rooms in our house had all of the furnishings they were supposed to have. Every inch of cupboard space in the kitchen was filled with plates, cups, appliances, and other kitcheny stuff. I had stylish containers on the counters. One to hold my collection of wooden spoons, one for the spatulas, and another for the whisks (all of them). The drawers and cabinets in our bathrooms were filled with pretty palettes and potions. The closets were wall to wall clothes, scarves, purses, and shoes that spilled into other rooms, even into the garage. All the space was filled. The funny thing is it didn't feel like too much until it did, and that's only because I was finally paying attention. Once I really opened my eyes to the clutter in my life, it was crushing. It was so heavy and I just wanted to be light.

In this section, we'll talk about making space, not just living space, but space for your heart to thrive, and space to create your life. At first I didn't think of my clutter as stress, but of course it was. It was a constant reminder of my debt and discontent. Think about how you feel when you walk into your home after a big day and there is paper all over the kitchen counter, your purse on the floor open and bursting at the seams, a pile of unfolded laundry, and odds and ends where they don't belong. The clutter and chaos on the outside make you feel cluttered and chaotic on the inside. You can't be at peace in that environment or give any thought to how you want to live. Instead, your thoughts are consumed with everything that needs to be done, and what has to get cleaned up or organized. Or, like I was in the beginning, you may be completely unaware of the impact your stuff and clutter has because you are so overwhelmed with everything else. Clutter attracts clutter and calm attracts calm. Once you decide which one you want more of, you can begin to thoughtfully create that for yourself.

While most of the changes I made happened one at a time, clearing the debt and the clutter simultaneously made sense. Because we were putting extra money toward debt, we weren't spending on new things. This gave us a chance to make real headway in making space. Other times I had tried to declutter, I just filled up the space I created with new stuff. This time was different. We needed the extra space we were creating. We needed more lightness. Because we were paying off tens of thousands of dollars in debt, that meant preparing for some hard conversations. Money, especially when you have a bunch of debt, can be stressful not only to deal with but to talk about. Less clutter resulted in more calm, so we could enter these conversations feeling less frazzled. I'm going to share with you how we talked about money issues as a couple and what happened when we started to be more open about what we wanted out of life.

I don't need to tell you how to declutter, but I will share some strategies that worked well for me. My way isn't the best way or the right way, but maybe it will help you get started. More important than the step-by-step of how to declutter your spaces, we are going to dig into the bigger picture: the why and the how did we get here, and the what can we learn so we never go back. Forget about spring cleaning, improving your organizational skills, and buying new stuff to store your stuff. I've got a better idea—because if organizing your stuff worked, you'd be organized by now.

CHAPTER NINE

The Myth of Ownership

A soulful simplicity isn't all peace and love and sitting quietly with your hands on your heart. Those are a few of the best parts, but we have to be logical too, and thoughtful about why we do what we do, so we can make changes that last. If you are tired of making the same mistakes over and over again, you'll be happy to know we are going to put an end to that here. The process of letting go will be much easier when you take the time to understand why you own what you own and how it got there in the first place. When I finally slowed down and noticed what was happening instead of racing for some imaginary, organized finished line, real change took hold of my heart. We buy and hold on to things for many reasons, but usually it's because we want to be someone we are not, feel something we don't, or prove we are something we don't think we are to someone else. I'm not opposed to owning things, but looking back, I see that everything I owned, owned me right back. See if you recognize why you own things in any of the following myths.

Myth #1: Aspirational Ownership

"If I own _____, I will be, look, or feel
_____."

For example:

"If I own a home, I will be a responsible adult."

"If I own a luxury car, I will be safe, comfortable, and appear to be affluent."

"If I own the latest tech device, I will be hip and cool and more productive."

"If I own the best face cream, I will look young."

"If I own the right containers and hangers, I will be organized."

"If I have the right suitcase, I'll be more adventurous and see the world."

"If I have a bigger table, I will entertain more often and have more friends."

"If I wear the right workout clothes, I'll go to the gym on a regular basis and get six-pack abs."

"If I wear the right shoes, people will think I'm powerful, sexy, and confident."

"If I buy the right stuff, I will fit in, I will be happy, and people will love me."

Unfortunately, we demonstrate over and over again that none of those statements are true. The hiking equipment still sits untouched in the garage, and the treadmill becomes a place to hang the clothes. The only truth of ownership is that when you own something, it owns you too. It's yours to take care of and pay for in every way every day.

Ownership begins with a purchase or investment of money. You make a down payment, swipe a little plastic, or pay with your hard-earned cash. After a momentary high (and often, subsequent low), you continue to pay for your ownership. You invest your time in taking care of the item. You direct energy toward thinking or worrying about what you own or how much money you spent on it. You spend more money protecting it and upgrading it. If you used a credit card, the item might not even be yours. It's possible that you are literally walking around in someone else's shoes because you're still paying them off, along with the addition of finance charges. I've been there. I was walking in other people's shoes for more than a decade.

Once we start looking at our stuff without filtering it through the lens of our expectations and emotions, we can see it for what it really is. It's just stuff. Aspirational ownership is buying things for the person you want to be or the lifestyle you wish you had. When you get rid of that stuff, you begin to understand who you are and what you truly want out of life. It's then that you can consider what you actually want or need. You can start purchasing for the right reasons when you find out you need and want less than you thought.

Myth #2: Pain-Avoidance Ownership

We buy things to make ourselves feel better. Even if you don't consider yourself a shopaholic, many shopping habits are compulsive and often circle back to avoiding pain. The pain may stem from:

Boredom. "There's nothing to do today, so let's go to the mall!" Have you ever said that? It starts out as a browsing adventure through stores to kill time, and then suddenly, you see something you didn't know you needed. And it's on sale! The truth is that you don't need to kill time at a mall. There are hiking trails, sidewalks, and indoor tracks for walking. There are mountains to climb. There is art to create, people to meet, and businesses to launch. When you get rid of your stuff, you can start to decide how you really want to spend your time, and the last thing you'll want to do is kill it at the mall. Shopping doesn't cure boredom. Curiosity does that.

Distractions/Procrastination. Instead of starting on the new project you've been thinking about or tackling a difficult conversation, you go to the nearest department store or shop online. Instead of decluttering, you go to a container store and buy more stuff for storing your stuff. There are hopes and dreams that you've had sitting on a shelf because you didn't have the time, money, or attention to get started. Shopping and other distractions stole some of that time, money, and attention. Plus, it takes energy to avoid what you truly want to do. Begin to notice when you use procrastination and distraction as a pain-avoidance tactic.

Ever shop post-breakup or after receiving bad news? Shopping may be soothing and it can provide a temporary lift and distraction from pain. What we have to remember, however, is that the distraction is always temporary, and the pain is often more severe when compounded with buyer's remorse. What else could you do to soothe your heartbreak? There are alternatives to shopping, booze, and ice cream to heal a broken heart. Could you spend some time with a loving friend, read one of your favorite books, take a long nap, or enjoy a walk in nature?

Guilt. After running crazy during a busy workweek and not giving the attention to people in your life who deserve it most, you might want to make it up to them by taking them out for an expensive dinner or for a little shopping spree. Sure, this will make them smile for a moment, but what they really want is you. They deserve more than stuff and so do you. Spending time with people you love doesn't have to cost anything.

There are many reasons to shop, but when you shift your love from stuff and things to people and passions, a day at the mall will be agony.

Myth #3: Just-in-Case Ownership

As you let go of your stuff, pay attention to the following three words, because they will come up a lot: Just. In. Case. Everyone's "just in case" items are different, but they might include or be similar to:

The fat or skinny clothes that do not fit "just in case" you gain or lose weight.

The plastic piece that fell off the back of your remote control or another random piece or part "just in case" you figure out where it belongs.

The key that hasn't belonged to any door or lock in recent history "just in case" it suddenly does.

The sweatshirt your ex left behind "just in case" you get back together.

Your ski poles, even though you live in the tropics, "just in case" you move back to the snow and take up skiing again.

These things might sound silly, but so will some of your own excuses. The reason we don't hear the silliness or senselessness of our just-in-case is because we don't finish the sentence. Instead of just saying, "I'm keeping this just in case," finish the sentence: "I'm keeping this just in case _____." Just in case what? Articulate what you think might happen. For more incentive, say it out loud and in front of other people. Joshua Millburn and Ryan Nicodemus, founders of theminimalists.com, created the 20/20 theory, proving that almost any "just in case" item that you get rid of can be replaced for less than twenty dollars in less than twenty minutes. You usually don't have to replace it, but knowing that should alleviate some of the anxiety of letting go. Use this theory to remove some of your fears about those pesky "just in case" items. When you realize you've been holding on to things for the wrong reasons, it will be easier to let go.

The just in case excuse for holding on is a messy combination of fear and procrastination. We hold on because we aren't quite ready to let go but we rarely use or enjoy the just in case stuff we keep. Take a look in the back of your closet, in the junk drawer, or in boxes in your garage or attic and it's clear that just in case means never. When we say, "I'll keep this just in case," what we are really saying is . . .

I'm not ready.
I'm afraid to let go.
I'm afraid I won't have enough.

For those of us decluttering and in search of more peace, our problem isn't "not enough." Too much is our issue. Just in case doesn't just apply to clutter and things in our home. What else is going on in your life that you are holding onto out of fear? Admitting that just in case means never allows us to stop procrastinating and invites us to let go and stop living in fear. When we say good-bye to just in case, we can start living and giving in more meaningful ways.

What is your myth? I've indulged in each of them. I never thought about the stuff I owned as stressful or damaging until I started to get rid of it and felt the weight of the stuff lifting from my life. Once you acknowledge why you buy and what you think your stuff is doing for you, you will be more intentional about what comes into your home and life, and you will have more clarity about what needs to go. Then, when you declutter, you won't just let go of a physical object. You will let go of all of the stress and myths attached to it. Without all of that, you can be free and light. Now that you understand the myths, you can acknowledge the truth about what you own now, and what you choose to own in the future.

CHAPTER TEN

Shopping Away the Pain

When I started getting rid of stuff and got serious about paying down the debt I had accrued over the years, I wondered what I'd do if I wasn't shopping. Shopping was a bit of a sport for me, not to mention the lift I got at the end of a hard day or week. I thought I loved shopping and I know I'm not alone. On more than one occasion, someone has approached me after a speaking event and said, "But I love shopping. What will I do if I'm not shopping?" My answer is . . . maybe you don't know what you love. That's what I discovered. I thought I loved shopping too. I didn't understand my relationship with shopping until I stopped shopping on a regular basis. I didn't love shopping or any of the things I purchased on my excursions. Instead, I loved the feeling of shopping. The relief. The distraction. I was shopping away the pain. Author and vulnerability researcher Brené Brown calls it numbing. Unfortunately, I wasn't just numbing the pain. Brown says, "We cannot selectively numb emotions; when we numb the painful emotions, we also numb the positive emotions." When I heard those words for the first time at an event in 2012, I thought, "Oh, so that's where the joy went." I was numbing that too. I didn't know what I loved because I was numbing out. And I called that love. I didn't love shopping, I loved numbing the pain.

So what was my pain? I had a good childhood. I never wanted for anything. I had a job, a roof over my head, people I loved. When I looked around me, my life seemed pretty good. The pain wasn't acute or based on one traumatic event, but instead it built slowly with every compromise I made, each time I said yes when I wanted to say no, every time I overcommitted, overspent, said "just a sec" to my daughter and made her wait an hour, made my phone my priority, did things because I thought I was supposed to, and each time I tried to prove my worth to someone else by what I accomplished, owned, or said. I thought my pain was just part of the dream. Danielle LaPorte, author of *The Desire Map*, said, "If you have to step outside of yourself, away from your values and soul to get your needs met, then you're not really going to get your needs met." I was constantly stepping outside of myself. That was my pain. I stepped out of myself so many times, I forgot who I was.

Shopping numbed the pain and it felt like an accomplishment. If you've ever found one of your favorite brand-name jackets or dresses for half price, you know what I mean. But after a few days, and definitely by the time the credit card statement came in, I felt terrible about my purchase. Luckily there was a quick fix for that pain too. A glass of wine, a pint of ice cream, or even more shopping. There was always a quick fix. More numbing. I sort of knew that's what was happening, but it felt easier to continue living the status quo than to address the problem.

Another question I'm frequently asked is "How do you deal with the pain now? If you get bored, frustrated, angry, and you can't satisfy the pain with shopping, what do you do?" When I stopped shopping for a while, instead of stuffing my feelings, I listened to them. Instead of shopping away pain or worry, I felt it. I started to understand that those feelings were my body's way of saying, "Listen, something's not right."

Now, when I am feeling pain, I take better care of myself. My heart is telling me it's time to make a change. When I'm not feeling my best, I know my body is saying, "Please take care of me," not "Let's go buy things."

INSTEAD OF GOING SHOPPING, I . . .

—Take a walk

—Go to yoga

—Call a friend

—Make a smoothie

—Get a massage

—Sleep for an extra hour

—Write

—Meditate

—Send a thank-you note

Those simple things provide more motivation, energy, and love than shopping ever did. I traded shopping for self-care.

Three Shopping Mantras

If you feel bad about buying something new, you are not alone. I have felt that way more times than I care to admit. Emotions and shopping go hand in hand. I shopped for the highs and the lows, and for new seasons and events, but I also shopped in the excitement of a new habit. If I joined a new gym with the intention of exercising more consistently, I'd buy new workout clothes and shoes. After a few months, I'd lose interest in the gym and shove my new clothes in the closet. Following that were the post-shopping emotions. I felt guilty for spending too much money, annoyed when something went on sale months after I bought it, and frustrated when things didn't fit right or change my life in any profound way.

As I began to change my ways and simplify my life, I discovered a few strategies that helped me take a good look at why I was shopping and helped me better define what I really wanted and needed. Keeping the following three statements in mind, I became much more intentional about shopping and about the stuff I decided to let into my home and my life.

1. **I don't have to buy this today.**

   I chose a purchase pause over impulse shopping. Instead of buying something, I literally paused. Try it. Put a pause on nonessential purchases. Instead of buying with your money, fake the purchase on paper. For thirty to sixty days, keep a running list of everything you want to buy with the price of each item, but don't actually buy anything. At the end of your purchase pause, add up what you would have spent and ask yourself these two questions:

Is there anything on the list I still want as much as I thought I did?

If someone handed me the total amount of my fake purchases in cash, would I use it to buy all the things on the list, or use it for something else?

This experiment will provide you with valuable information to consider before future purchases. After thirty to sixty days, consider a full-on shopping ban. Canadian author Cait Flanders didn't buy anything new for two years with the exception of a few items on her approved shopping list—not even take-out coffee. Here's what Cait had to say as she reflected on her first year of no shopping.

The entire journey forced me to give up all the things we are taught to want in life: the newest and greatest of this, that or the other. I exchanged them for basic necessities and, after a year of not being able to buy anything new, I've realized I have all I could ever need. I don't value material objects anymore. I value people, places, and experiences. This new mind-set has not only saved me money, it's expanded my capacity to care for others and to find gratitude in the simplest things. And perhaps the best outcome of all is that I will never again purchase something because I want to portray a certain level of success or character quality I wish I had.

2. I can return that.

Almost everything you purchase can be returned. If you bought something recently that is weighing you down financially or emotionally, return it. If it's too late to return it, give it away, or sell it. Don't hold on to something that makes you feel bad. I don't recommend using this as an excuse to keep buying, but as an invitation to let yourself off the hook if you did buy something you don't want or need. Sometimes, especially if you are just going through the motions, or stuck in a pattern of shopping to feel your way out of feeling, or holding on to things out of guilt, it's hard to detect the real hold that stuff and shopping have on you. Once you begin to simplify, you will begin to see how your shopping and spending habits are really affecting your life.

3. I have paid enough.

Realizing I had paid enough changed everything for me. Now, I don't hold on to guilt or feel bad about my past purchase transgressions. I already paid. I paid with my money, my time, my attention, and my emotions. There is no benefit or need for me to keep paying. Accepting the fact that I had paid enough allowed me to cut the ties between emotion, shopping, and holding on. With that simple truth, I finally let go. Haven't you paid enough too?

CHAPTER ELEVEN

Is This Love

I used to have a goal of buying a new pair of sunglasses in every city I visited. Acquiring a new pair of sunglasses was a primary focus of almost every trip I took for a few years. I'm not proud of that meaningless goal, but I'm sharing it to demonstrate that I had a long way to go from the person I was pretending to be then to remembering who I was and living a soulful simplicity. Sunglasses weren't my only weakness when it came to stuff. I had collections of purses, cosmetics, scarves, coats, and it was never enough. The more I had, the more I wanted. I used to fool myself into believing that one more thing would complete or enhance my existing collection in some way. Of course, it never did.

If you want to live with less stuff, decluttering is only half the battle. The rest depends on what you bring home, and for those of us who have a habit of shopping, this is often the harder part. I had to stop shopping for a while to really understand how destructive it was in my life. For a really long time, I thought I deserved nice things, new things, anything I wanted. The truth is, I deserve so much more than stuff.

When I had a closet full of clothes, I never experienced the deep gratitude I have when I look at a small selection of my favorite things now. The same goes for the rest of my house. When I "had it all" I wanted more. Now that I own less, I am more grateful because what I own contributes to a happier, healthier life instead of taking away from it.

I need way less than I thought to be happy. My constant quest for more resulted in frustration, overspending, and discontent. You may think you need certain things in life to be successful or happy, but I recommend continually challenging your thoughts around that. Really think about how you want to spend your days, your hours, your minutes, and your moments. It's hard to believe that adding a few items from the clothing section at Target every weekend when I was grocery shopping was affecting the way I spent my time, but were I to add it all up and combine it with all of the other "little" purchases, it did. It does. It all matters. Now I choose love over stuff. People I love, work I love, and a life I love. When I started letting go of stuff and freeing up space I had no idea how connected to love this journey is. Section four of this book is all about love, and had I known that was the path from the beginning, letting go would have been much easier for me.

Stay Focused on Your Own Stuff

If you are ready to let go, but your spouse or other family members are not, it might be frustrating. The most powerful thing you can do is stay focused on your own stuff. Have gentle conversations about things you own together, but don't worry about your husband's closet, or your roommate's cluttered space. When you feel tempted to "get people on board," consider the last time someone tried to persuade you to make a change you weren't ready for. Did you feel excited, or annoyed? Motivated or pressured? Let the people in your life find their own way, just as you are finding yours. If you want others to see the joy in less, live joyfully with less.

How I Let Go

I used to declutter twice a year, once to ring in the new year and again in the spring. I did it to "get organized" and "start fresh," but really I was just making room for new stuff. I know this only because my get-organized, start-fresh cycle had to be repeated at least twice a year. When I finally decided to declutter for good, my methods didn't change much, but my intention did. This time I was getting rid of things to make room for something much more important than more stuff. This time, with each thing I let go of, I let go of a piece of stress and made room to figure out what I really cared about, and how I wanted to fill my space and spend my time. I didn't have a goal in mind of how much I wanted to get rid of, but my plan was to just keep going until what was left was only what I used or enjoyed. That meant letting go of the "just in case," the "I spent so much on that," the "but someone who loves me gave me that," and even the sentimental stuff, the stuff I had saved since I was old enough to save things. My "decluttering for good" started with a simple pass around my house with a box. I filled it with all the things that I barely even noticed from day to day, or didn't use or appreciate. Things like vases, empty picture frames, clothes that didn't fit, and duplicate sets of measuring cups and glassware. Then I waited. I waited to see if I would miss anything and to see if my space felt any different. It did. I couldn't really tell what wasn't there anymore, but I definitely noticed what was starting to appear: space and light. There was so much more light. That encouraged me to take another pass, and another and another. It became easier and easier to let go. Then it got hard again when I got to things I thought I cared about. Things like books, jewelry, journals, and other things that felt precious. So I gave it more time. I let my new space and perspective work on my heart.

Reset to Zero

Once you begin to declutter, you may notice clutter trying to creep back in, or you might not notice until it's already crept. Either way, it's helpful to develop a practice to keep clutter at bay. Author Colin Wright suggests a weekly reset to zero.

Here's how he describes his practice:

At least once a week, I like to reset to zero.

I wash the dishes, drying each piece of flatware and cutlery until it's ready to be tucked away into its respective cabinet. Laundry is done. Anything scattered about the floor is picked up and put in its proper place, the floor is mopped or vacuumed. Every surface is cleared of clutter, the trash taken out; my entire home reset to its resting state. My inbox is zeroed—every message is either deleted or acted upon and archived. My to-do list lacks any items of immediate concern. My life—and my environment—becomes a nice, malleable, lump of clay. Dull, in a way, because it's been rendered shapeless by the lack of excess, clutter, or responsibility, for the moment. But exciting because it has unlimited potential. With little effort, I can reshape it into anything. With even less I can sit and look at it, all variables and rough edges momentarily smooth, allowing me to get a clear, unfettered idea of how best to proceed. I find that allowing myself to reset also allows me to clear my internal clutter—to recalibrate and figure out where to go next, what project to focus on, or what book to settle in with, comfortable knowing that all loose ends have been tied off, if only for a little while.

Resetting to zero is kind of a one-off version of minimalism, if you think about it. A minimalist refocuses her life on what's important by eschewing excess and homing in on what's most important to her. Resetting to zero allows you to do the same on a different scale for a period of time. You needn't get rid of the things that don't bring you value to reset to zero, and you still get a taste of what life could feel like, all the time, if you ever decided to. Even better, if you do find yourself taking a minimalist leap someday, resetting to zero can become even more valuable; it becomes that much easier to apply. When you own only the most vital of possessions and occupy a space that makes sense for you and your needs, you'll find it takes all of 10–15 minutes to reset to zero, giving you a quick and easy way to clear your mental tablet and start from scratch. Like minimalism, resetting to zero is not about going without; you don't lack for anything by having your home tidy and your dishes done. Resetting is about seeing how clearly you're able to think when all the little stresses of the day are neutralized. It's about re-centering yourself and having the time and presence of mind to deep-dive into who you are, what you want, and in what direction you're currently moving. It's about being happier and more fulfilled, and achieving both goals by giving yourself the chance to change direction quickly, and with few negative consequences, should such a change be warranted.

The first step of any journey can be the most difficult. Thankfully, resetting to zero only asks that you do the dishes.

Is This Love?

When I think about spending on something new I don't really need, or am trying to decide if I should keep something or let it go (physical object, commitment, work project . . .), I ask this one simple (yet really big) question: Is this love? Does this support love in my life the way I want it to? If the answer is no, I walk away. If the answer is yes, I wait and ask the question a few days or weeks later. Most of the time my yes turns to no and I realize whatever I wanted in that moment wasn't love. Try it for yourself. It helps to ask the questions out loud.

"Does this really matter to me?"

"Is this love?"

"Is this contributing to the life I want, to my health, or to the way I want to treat people?"

"Am I holding on for the right reasons?"

We will revisit these questions at the end of the section. Ask them about your stuff, about how you feel, about your work, about a grudge, about everything. Put your hands on your heart and ask. Your heart knows things and she will help you make room for what matters most.

CHAPTER TWELVE

The Magic of Letting Go

We all have an ugly coffee mug, a framed picture on the wall that we walk by every day without noticing, or a scarf that, while treasured, is never worn. Even though a clutter-free life sounds appealing, some things are harder to let go of than others. We may each hold on to different items, but we experience a similar struggle in terms of the hold our things have on us. When letting go, it helps to start with the easy stuff like duplicates, and things you know you won't miss—strengthening your decluttering muscles. I recommend taking a first pass around your entire home with a big box, filling it with the things you know you don't really appreciate or care about. Once the box is full, and it won't take long, tape it up and donate it. Then take some time before your next pass to enjoy the space you've created. In most cases, it will take only a few days to forget what you put in the box. That stuff didn't matter at all.

Once you build your decluttering muscles, you'll have an easier time when it comes to the more challenging things, but there may still be a few items that have a hold on your heart. Our heart strings are strong, but the following recommendations will help you get rid of clutter you care about, or you think you care about. There isn't one tried-and-true approach for anyone, so approach your decluttering with curiosity and see what works for you. I even discovered there wasn't just one approach for me. I had to try different things at different times.

Hide It

This is one of the most effective strategies for seeing what kind of value, if any, an item adds to your life. During our early stages of decluttering, Mark and I had three vases on our bedroom bureau, each holding a flower that represented the flowers at our wedding. Sounds meaningful, right? They were lovely, but I realized I noticed them only when I was dusting them, or accidentally knocking one over. I wanted to see what it would be like to live without them. Because we had already cleared out so much, they were the last of the decorative items in our bedroom and the only things that sat on top of the bureau. I wrapped them up, placed them in a box, and put the box in the garage. I wondered if I would miss them, or how long it would take before I wanted to put them back.

I didn't mention my little experiment to my husband. I kept waiting for him to ask about them, but he never did, and after a few days, even I forgot about my treasured vases. Two months later I went into the garage, unpacked the box with the vases and set them up on the bureau as if they had never been gone. One night, before we fell asleep, I pointed to the vases and told Mark I wanted to donate them and he said, "No, I really like those." I had to laugh a little bit. When I told him they'd been in the garage for months, he laughed too and agreed it was a good time to let them go. Since then, whenever I travel for work and Mark stays home, something goes missing. If I can't figure out what it is, out the door it goes. I love this little ritual we've created.

A little separation goes a long way when it comes to parting with your stuff. It's why I recommend that people who try minimalist fashion challenge Project 333 (I'll tell you more about it in chapter 15) put excess clothing out of sight for three months instead of donating it immediately. It eliminates the fear of missing something or the fear of not having enough and determines if it's really our hearts holding on, or whether it's fear that is encouraging the tight grip.

Question It

Use Marie Kondo's suggestion from *The Life-Changing Magic of Tidying Up* and question your stuff. She says to hold each item in your hand and ask, "Does this bring me joy?" Additionally, I recommend creating a list of the moments that make you most joyful, and when you ask your item if it brings you joy, compare it with your list. Does it make the list, or even come close? If the answer is no, let it go and, as Kondo says, be grateful for how the item served you.

Keep It

There isn't any magic in getting rid of everything. If the ugly coffee cup makes you smile every morning, keep it. If your spouse wants to keep their ugly coffee mug, let them enjoy it. Put your stuff through the tests above, and if you determine that you want it in your life, make space for it and appreciate it.

We cannot compare or measure our lives based on what we do or do not own. That line of thinking doesn't make any sense. One of my yoga teachers told me about the first time he touched his toes after years of practicing yoga and thinking he wasn't flexible enough. After he finally connected fingers to toes he realized not much had changed. Touching his toes was supposed to be this monumental moment, but what he noticed was that he was just a little more flexible. Nothing else had changed.

How to Let Go of the Guilt of Letting Go

We each have our own reasons for holding on to stuff, clutter, negative emotions, and other things. Usually, all of our excuses, fears, and resistance come back to a few common struggles. One of those struggles is guilt. The problem with guilt is that instead of helping us change our behavior, it usually keeps us in a holding pattern.

I remember feeling guilt when I looked in my closet and saw clothes I never wore purchased with money I didn't have. I felt guilty when I said no to people, or even when I thought about saying no. I felt guilty about thinking about letting go of gifts or things other people gave me. I felt guilty about overdue credit card bills and collection calls, guilt for shopping to feel better, for feeling less than enough because I didn't own the right things, or have the right car/shoes/kitchen . . . and the list goes on and on.

I even felt guilty for rejecting all the things I thought I always wanted. This guilt wasn't all-consuming, but it surfaced more when I made the decision to start slowing down and letting go. I finally had the time and space to feel all the feelings. If you struggle with guilt too, try this:

1. **Own the guilt.**

   If you feel guilty every time you open your closet and see an expensive dress hanging with the tags still on, or a pair of shoes that give you blisters, own the guilt. Write it down. That flash of guilt you may experience on a daily basis has become so consistent, it feels normal. What you may have forgotten, though, is that it is your choice to carry the burden of feeling guilty about what's in your closet, or other areas of your home. It's your choice (this was a tough one for me).

2. Reject the guilt.

I used to think I was supposed to feel guilty. After all, with all the mistakes I made, shouldn't a bit of guilt go along with them? What I didn't know is that the guilt was weighing me down with absolutely no purpose. The guilt wasn't serving me in any way. When I recognized that guilt had become an anchor, instead of inspiring something better, it was easier to let it go. Remember: we have paid enough.

3. Let it flow.

Brooke McAlary runs *The Slow Home Podcast* in Australia. She was addressing a question about gifts during a webinar we hosted together, and I often pass on this brilliant advice she gave. Someone asked, "What should I do if I am trying to live with less and people give me gifts I don't want?" Brooke said, "Simply let them flow through your home." In other words, accept the gifts with love and then let them go. Brooke and I knew the question wasn't really about what to do with the gifts, but instead what to do with the guilt, so I added, "Let the guilt flow out with the gifts."

The biggest gift of gifts is in the exchange. It's in the "I'm thinking of you" or the "I love you" and not what's contained in the gift box. Is there really any "thing" someone could give you to prove their love? It doesn't happen like that. Love isn't a one-time gift. It doesn't arrive wrapped perfectly, and you never have to prove it.

Joshua Becker, author of *The More of Less,* once told me, "It's important to receive the gift with the intention it was given." For some people, giving gifts is the way they express their love, but again the real gift isn't in the package. The real gift is happening during the exchange. Give yourself permission to accept the love and let the rest flow. Letting it flow doesn't just apply to gifts. When you let go of anything in your life that doesn't add value, let the guilt flow with it. The best way to let go of the guilt of letting go is to let joy replace the guilt. Let love replace the guilt. You have a limited amount of space and time in your life and if you fill it all with guilt and regret, there won't be room for all of the love. Remind yourself that you simply don't have room in your life for guilt.

I still give and receive gifts at Christmas, but focus on experiences over stuff. And I put presence before presents. I've learned that you can't buy other people's love with gifts. You have to show up for love.

The Guilt of Letting Go Doesn't Come from Letting Go

When stuff becomes a constant reminder of debt or discontent, we feel bad, sad, and guilty. When I look back, I can clearly see that guilt was just as much a part of my clutter as the things hanging in my closet or the stuff in my junk drawers. I also know that the guilt and the stuff were deeply connected and when I let go of the stuff, the guilt went with it. What's interesting about the guilt of letting go is that the guilt doesn't usually come from letting go. It comes from holding on. When guilt is attached to holding on, the only remedy is to let go. I could continue to feel guilt about past mistakes, about my past debt, clutter, and busyness. Instead, I've let it go so I can live today with purpose and joy.

My journey to a soulful simplicity is similar to my yoga teacher's journey to touch his toes. When it comes to what you own, there is no magic number of items to sacrifice in order to feel lighter. There are lessons in letting go and major benefits along the way, just like in stretching and yoga, but be gentle with yourself and mindful about how living more simply is changing you and bringing you closer to what matters most. The magic in reaching for your toes happens when you feel the stretch, wherever that may be. The magic in letting go happens when you feel light, wherever that may be.

CHAPTER THIRTEEN

Your Money or Your Life

If I made a list of the most stressful things in my life, money would have been at the top from when I turned eighteen and got my first credit card until my late thirties when Mark and I decided to become debt-free. We were tired of making all of our decisions based on money. The heavy, stressful feeling that came from our debt began to lift as soon as we made the decision to pay down the debt. We had years of work ahead of us, but by simply choosing a better path, we felt lighter. We both brought some debt into the marriage, but I brought most of it—student loans, a car loan, credit cards, old medical bills. Add that to our home mortgage and everything we were spending to make our house a home, and it's easy to see how we were living beyond our means. Because we were eliminating stress to live a happier, healthier life, even with my MS, we decided to work together to pay off all of our debt. We knew this would involve taking a close look at what we actually owed, that we'd have to have conversations about money that we usually avoided, and a change of lifestyle would be in order, at least for a little while. I started the process by rereading the one book that had me considering a change years before my diagnosis, *Your Money or Your Life* by Vicki Robin and Joe Dominguez. I often read books before and during a big change for extra inspiration, motivation, and to strengthen my resolve, so it was the perfect time to revisit this book that once had my heart's attention. I think the reason this book's message resonated with me is because it approached the topic of money not from a math perspective, but with a focus on lifestyle and behavior. If mastering money was all about the numbers, I knew I was in trouble.

The premise of *Your Money or Your Life* is that many of us are trading our lives for money in how we spend our days, as in this example shared in the book:

> *Consider the average worker in almost any urban industrialized city. The alarm rings at 6:45 and our working man or woman is up and running. Shower. Dress in the professional uniform—suits or dresses for some, coveralls for others, whites for the medical professionals, jeans and flannel shirts for construction workers. Breakfast, if there's time. Grab a commuter mug and briefcase (or lunch box). Hop in the car for the daily punishment called rush hour or on a bus or train packed crushingly tight. On the job from nine to five. Deal with the boss. Deal with the coworker sent by the devil to rub you the wrong way. Deal with suppliers. Deal with clients/customers/patients. Act busy. Hide mistakes. Smile when handed impossible deadlines. Give a sigh of relief when the ax known as "restructuring" or "downsizing"—or just plain getting laid off—falls on other heads. Shoulder the added workload. Watch the clock. Argue with your conscience but agree with the boss. Smile again. Five o'clock.*

Back in the car and onto the freeway or into the bus or train for the evening commute. Home. Act human with mates, kids or roommates. Eat. Watch TV. Bed. Eight hours of blessed oblivion.

This might not be your picture, but many of us have experienced a version of it, including checking e-mail and Facebook every five minutes. I know how it feels to do work you don't enjoy to earn money to pay for all the things you need to make yourself feel better for doing work you don't enjoy. The career or life path you chose at twenty may not resonate at thirty or forty or beyond. But we keep trying to make it work because by then we feel stuck. We have to keep making money to maintain our lifestyles and try to convince ourselves we are making a life and not just a paycheck. I had no intention of quitting my job when we began our debt-free journey, but as each debt disappeared and we reduced our financial obligations, I knew it was a possibility. There are several powerful exercises in *Your Money or Your Life* that expose some harsh truths about what you really earn, how you are trading what they call your life energy for stuff, and how to make concrete changes. The lessons from *Your Money or Your Life* helped me in many ways, but when it was time for a hard plan for how we would pay off our debt, we turned to author and radio host Dave Ramsey. We wanted a proven strategy that wasn't rooted in "get rich quick" philosophy, and it worked for us. Dave shares on his Web site that 78 percent of Americans live paycheck to paycheck and 90 percent are buying things they can't afford. We fell into both of those statistics. We joined his program, Financial Peace University, offered at many local churches and online, and started with step one, "Put $1,000 in an emergency fund." At first that sounded crazy to me. Why would I save up $1,000 for emergencies when I could use it to pay down my debt? Then again, what I was doing wasn't working, so I decided to follow the rules.

It took us a few years to pay off all of our debt, and putting in that time changed many of our other behaviors including overspending, recreational shopping, and buying things we thought we were supposed to have. The better I felt, the less I cared about upgrading appliances, buying new carpet for the living room, or building a new deck or fence. We started talking more about what was important to us, and what kind of life we wanted to have, how we wanted to support our daughter, and what life would look like when we were debt-free. I struggled sometimes when I fought with my old habits of just spending whatever I wanted, but I also noticed that I was more at peace spending less, and owing and owning less. I certainly didn't miss the shopping hangovers and buyer's remorse. We followed Dave Ramsey's advice and paid our smallest debts first. Some disagree with this approach and suggest paying your biggest debts with the highest interest rates. Ramsey says, "Controlling your money isn't a math problem. It's a behavior problem. The best way to beat debt isn't to break out a slide rule and an abacus; you have to change the way you think about money." We weren't trying to game the system, find better interest rates, or even improve our credit scores. We just wanted to be free.

I found Dave Ramsey on the radio. Listening to people, regular people like me, call in with questions about finances and sharing their debt-free stories was inspiring. I thought, "If they can do it, so can I." I also loved Ramsey's no-nonsense approach. We attacked our debt from all angles. We socked away $1,000 in an emergency fund, mostly to ward off emergencies, and then started throwing extra money at our debts, smallest to largest. I cut up all my cards (the ends). I remembered how empowered I felt calling company after company resisting their new enticing offers for better rates and more points. It was a little scary. What if I needed a credit card for an emergency? And then I thought about my emergency fund and all of my nonemergency credit card "emergency" purchases. We started buying anything we needed with cash and stopped buying all the things we didn't really need. We also sold some of our things and put the extra money toward debt. We had a $50 rule for selling our stuff. If we thought we could sell something for $50 or more, we did, and if it was less than that we gave it away. Our time was valuable too so we didn't want to spend it haggling over $10 items. Once we were debt-free, we stopped selling things and gave them away. We had what I like to call our "last yard sale ever" and had a local charity scheduled to pick up whatever we didn't sell. We gave Bailey the option to sell her stuff too and keep and use the money. She had a station at the yard sale with her stuffed animals and clothes she didn't wear. Every penny we earned went toward the debt, and all of the leftover stuff we donated. We've never had another yard sale. When we sold our house, there were things we didn't know what to do with, so we just put it all in the driveway and posted a picture of the whole lot online with our address and two simple words: "Free stuff." It was gone in less than an hour.

Redefining Success

Because I worked in sales for so long, I measured success in deadlines and dollars. I measured myself by how much I accomplished, and how much I had. I compared and competed my way to bigger numbers and more stuff, but it had no meaningful impact on my life. I forgot to include the rest of my life in my success equation and instead kept it all focused on money and stuff. Mistake #3,249.

The benefits I was experiencing as I was simplifying my life plus information from books and other bloggers inspired me to reconsider my definition of success. I had started my blog, *Be More with Less*, while we were paying down debt and selling and giving away our stuff and connected with other bloggers who were discovering the joy of less too. I remember thinking maybe I should wait until I had things all figured out, until we were debt-free, or until I was more of an expert to start blogging, but then I realized the people who inspired me weren't experts, they were going through it and figuring it out. They didn't know it all. They were just sharing their stories, the highs and the lows. There was Tammy Strobel. In 2005, she and her husband Logan were overwhelmed with debt and clutter, and neither of them were happy in their jobs. They decided to simplify. They got rid of 90 percent of their stuff, built and lived in a tiny house on wheels, became debt-free, and changed their careers. Tammy is one of the most kindhearted people I know, in great part due to getting rid of so much stress. Leo Babauta started his transformation in Guam. He's a husband and dad to six children. Before he decided to simplify his life, he was unhappy and unhealthy. He was deep in debt and eased his pain by smoking and overeating. I watched as he documented his journey of total transformation. Today he lives in California with his children and wife Eva. They got rid of most of their stuff, all of their debt, and Leo quit smoking, dropped the extra weight, created his own business, adopted a healthier, vegan diet, and runs daily. And there were more. Joshua Becker, husband, pastor, and dad, decided to live more simply after spending a frustrating afternoon cleaning out his garage instead of spending time with his son. Joshua Fields Millburn partnered with his childhood friend Ryan Nicodemus to start a blog about minimalism after losing his mother to cancer and getting divorced in the same year and realizing that there had to be more to life. After seeing how minimalism was changing their lives and the lives of the people they were reaching through their Web site, Joshua and Ryan created *Minimalism*, a documentary about the important things.

Each of their stories encouraged my journey and showed me that your story doesn't have to be perfect or complete to inspire others. After all, perfect isn't real. We cannot connect with, or be moved or changed by perfection. For a long time, I thought I'd never get it together, or that I couldn't help others because I was such a mess, or that sharing my story would waste other people's time because it wasn't good enough, perfect enough, or powerful enough. The late Leonard Cohen knew otherwise: "There is a crack in everything. That's how the light gets in."

My new definition of success includes metrics like how I spend my time, and how I treat people, including myself. It has nothing to do with deadlines, dollars, stuff, square footage, or job titles anymore.

CHAPTER FOURTEEN

A Simple Invitation

As we've established and as many of you have experienced, money can be stressful, and talking about it is even more stressful, especially when there is more month at the end of the money. Mark and I were doing great working our way through paying down our debt. There were so many changes I wanted to make, but I didn't know how Mark felt. I didn't want to force him into change or to do it completely on my own. I wanted the changes I had in mind to bring us closer, not divide us. He was always really good about entertaining my decluttering ideas, but I'm not sure if he knew what I had in mind next. I wanted to keep going, to keep living small so we could live big.

I'd drop a few hints over dinner, or before one of us left for work, but I knew if I wanted him to seriously consider something different, we had to have a conversation that couldn't really happen on the fly. I had to create a time and place where we could focus on a conversation that could potentially change our lives. I remember e-mailing him an invitation to join me at our first "Simplicity Summit"—maybe it was a little dorky to give it a name like that, but I wanted there to be some fun and lightheartedness around all of the serious things we'd be talking about. I thought a Simplicity Summit would be a good place to start. I wanted to create an environment where we could talk about things that might make us uncomfortable in a supportive way.

Our First Simplicity Summit

We had been talking about having our Simplicity Summit for a few weeks and decided to set the date. I e-mailed Mark during the day to remind him and let him know how excited I was to talk about us and our lives. That set the tone. This wasn't going to be a doom-and-gloom chat, this was going to be an awesome conversation about our lives. Before our meeting we went for a thirty-minute walk to completely unwind and leave the workday behind us. When we got home we sat at the kitchen table with our laptops. I created a document online that we could both review and edit as we were talking. Any document would have worked, even pen and paper as long as we could both easily read and work on it at the same time. The digital document was nice, though, because it was easy to revisit. The first thing we reviewed was our why. Why were we taking the time to do this? We typed this at the top of the document: "We are holding this Simplicity Summit to review monthly bills, a savings plan, to consider the idea of moving and downsizing to a smaller home, to talk about how things are and how we want things to be. Now that we are open to living unconventionally, this conversation will help us move forward." Our document and discussion were broken up into five sections: money, health, questions/discussion, where do we want to be, and action steps.

1. Money

We started with the bills. We wanted to jump right in. By identifying some clear talking points, we eliminated the emotion that often surrounds money and could talk about the facts. We reviewed a list of monthly expenses and put notes next to any item with questions or ideas to reduce or eliminate it. We also reviewed other expenses including groceries, dining out, travel, sports, household, etc. Our big question after reviewing the two lists was "How can we cut more of our expenses and intentionally save and give more?"

2. Health

We met our max out-of-pocket and deductible (thank you, multiple sclerosis) with our health insurance, so any services completed by the end of the year would be covered at 100 percent. We listed any appointments that could be made and added them to the action steps below. Instead of my nagging Mark to make an appointment for a physical every day for the next two weeks, it's on his list. I'm also more likely to schedule my appointments because I know I'm accountable.

Health had to be part of this discussion because after all a health scare is what got us here in the first place. It was important to both of us to take care of ourselves so we could bring our best to each other. That doesn't mean we were always in perfect health or making perfectly healthy decisions, but we were taking care of ourselves so we could better take care of each other and our daughter.

3. Questions/Discussion

I started a list of questions in advance of the meeting, and we both added answers and more questions. It was important to have them in writing because the next time we reviewed, we could see our initial reactions and ideas. Knowing that life will toss us curveballs, and being so happy with changes that we've made in our life, we were ready to talk about anything. We are happier when we are proactive instead of waiting for something to force our hand. Here are some of the questions that came up during our first summit:

* What stuff can we sell now?
* What will we sell when we move?
* What else can we give away?
* What do we need to do to sell our house?
* Why wait to sell the house?
* Why sell it now?
* What kind of home do we want to live in?
* What kind of community do we want to live in?
* How will we pay for college?
* Other ways to generate income?
* Should I take a part-time job?
* What do we need to do to plan for the holidays?
* What are our travel plans for the next year?
* Could we sell one car and share the other?
* Are there volunteer/service projects that we want to do in the community?

4. Where do we want to be?

We knew our lives were going to change significantly over the next year. We also admitted that we can't control everything, or much of anything, but we want to have some things to strive for.

One year: Max out emergency fund and figure out a loan-free college plan for Bailey.

Five years: Cut living expenses by 50 percent.

Ten years: We left this blank because we really don't know what our lives will look like in ten years. Things are changing all the time, and we want to be open to opportunity and serendipity.

5. Action steps (these were the action steps from our first simplicity summit; they change every time we do this)

Mark
- Make dentist appointment
- Make doctor's appointment
- Research car sale
- Car maintenance
- Set up automatic monthly savings deposit

Courtney
- Compare insurance rates
- Research scholarships/grants
- Schedule mammogram
- Start conversation with realtor

We met two weeks later to review our progress on the action steps. We could get by without Simplicity Summits, but we want to say the things that go unsaid and ask the questions that typically go unasked. That first Simplicity Summit was in 2012, before we sold our house, before our daughter graduated from high school, and even before I quit my job. We've had many since then and continue to intentionally talk about the lives we want. We talk about the fun stuff, and the hard stuff. My favorite topics always come from the question "Wouldn't it be crazy if we . . ." We are living our lives with purpose and it makes for a happy marriage and meaningful life together.

If you want to give this a try but the word *simplicity* is too intimidating, call it the Happiness Summit, or the Connection Summit. This meeting is about starting a conversation about your lives together.

HOW TO HAVE YOUR OWN SIMPLICITY SUMMIT

- Set the date. Choose a time when you can have an hour or two with no kids or distractions.
- Make an agenda. Come prepared with a list of questions and other information to review so you can spend time talking instead of researching.
- Have a conversation. Talk and then listen. Then listen more.
- Daydream a bit. Say things like "Wouldn't it be crazy if . . ." or "I think it would be awesome if we . . ." Then support the dreams, redefine them, and make them actionable.
- Ask questions like "Why now?" or "Why not now?" Play both sides of the coin to work through fears you may have that you didn't know about.

- Write it down.
- Clearly identify action steps for each person.
- Set the date for another quick accountability meeting in a week or two to review progress on the action steps.
- Always close the meeting with "Is there anything that we didn't cover that you want to talk about?"

You can hold a Simplicity Summit with your spouse, your family, or even by yourself. If you live alone, you can hold a solo Simplicity Summit. Regardless of age or any circumstance, it's important to intentionally and regularly review finances, health, and other things that are meaningful to you. Consistently observing and questioning the way you live and entertaining new opportunities and directions will lead to more questions, better answers, and living a life that is in line with your hopes, dreams, and values, and not the hopes, dreams, and values you think other people expect of you. The opportunity to grow, change, and thrive all depends on what you are willing to consider.

CHAPTER FIFTEEN

Simple Is the New Black

As I was simplifying my stuff, there was one area of my home I ignored for a while . . . my closet. I just didn't want to go there. My closet was the one place where I could continue to pick up a thing or two here and there, and after all, clothing was a need. We need to wear clothes. By the time I decided to include the closet in my simplicity journey, I knew I couldn't lean into this one. A slow approach to decluttering my closet wasn't going to work. There were decades of clothes stuffed not only in my closet but in drawers, boxes in the garage, and other spaces in my home. I decided to go all in and create a challenge for myself.

I started minimalist fashion challenge Project 333 in 2010 when I decided to figure out what I really wanted and needed in my closet. I challenged myself to dress with thirty-three items or less for three months including clothing, jewelry, accessories, and (this is where I lose most people) . . . shoes. I didn't count underwear, sleepwear, around the house loungewear, or workout gear. That said, to count as workout clothes, my workout clothes had to work out. My yoga pants had to go to yoga. If they were spending more time at the grocery store or out running errands, they would count toward the thirty-three items. I shared my idea about dressing with less online. Some people thought it sounded crazy. Some people thought I was crazy, and some people wanted to join in. At first, there were about a hundred other people who said, "I'm in." They left comments on the blog post and said they were going to do the challenge too. Some of them wanted to share their experience on their own blogs or social media. It was great to have a support system right from the start.

About a month into the challenge, I got a call from a reporter at the Associated Press who wanted to write about Project 333. The story was published in hundreds of newspapers and Web sites around North America and beyond. It was exciting to have my challenge out in the world, but scary too! I was still learning about dressing with less and certainly didn't consider myself an expert in the capsule wardrobe arena.

Severe

The response wasn't all positive. A *Vogue* marketing director was quoted in an article describing Project 333 as "severe and not for most people." Some may have dismissed the challenge as weird, crazy, or impossible as a result, even though plenty of people have discovered otherwise. Call it weird or crazy, but not severe. Dressing with less isn't a sacrifice, and surprisingly, the challenge isn't that challenging for most. What's severe is we are spending money we don't have on clothes we don't wear. The way we assess our value with our jean size and our self-worth with our net worth is severe, and the fast fashion trend is severe.

Project 333 started with a personal challenge to end closet chaos and further define what "enough" really means to me. One hundred people joined in and one reporter took interest. Since the beginning of the fashion challenge in 2010, so much has changed. A simple closet didn't just change my wardrobe, it changed my whole life. I've completely redefined my relationship with stuff and shopping.

There were the easy-to-identify outside changes:

* My mornings were easier.
* I got ready on time.
* I had more free time.
* I saved money.
* I was getting more compliments.

And then there were the more meaningful, life-changing inside shifts. I felt lighter with less guilt and decision fatigue. Seeing all the money I spent on clothing I didn't wear or enjoy every day wore me down. When the stuff went, the guilt went with it. I had more attention for things I really cared about. Now that my weekends weren't consumed with shopping, and I wasn't searching the Internet for the best deal, I had time to consider what my real interests were. I began to find confidence in who I was instead of what I wore. I always thought I needed something new to wear to be confident. I needed the right heels to feel powerful, or a new dress to feel sexy, or a new jacket to feel put together and prepared. I felt all of those things and more without anything new.

Tens of thousands have now participated from around the world, and since the first AP story appeared, Project 333 has been featured on the BBC, CNN, Today.com, and in *O: The Oprah Magazine*, *Real Simple*, and *More*. The most interesting observation I've made about the entire process, based on feedback from people who have dressed with thirty-three items or less, is that in the end, this fashion project has very little to do with fashion or clothes and much more to do with health, happiness, and lots of heart.

Simple Is the New Black

"Simple is the new black" wasn't always my fashion philosophy. When I was thirteen years old, my mom took me to Boston for an appointment with an orthopedic surgeon. I struggled with knee issues, so we had frequent trips to the city. The doctor visits were scary and sometimes painful, but my mom always made these trips something to look forward to. She'd take me out to lunch, to get my hair done, or we'd go shopping. I loved that those trips were just for the two of us to spend time together. One time, she took me to the iconic Filene's Basement in Boston. I saw two grown women, half dressed in the middle of the store, fighting over a discounted brand-name dress. I looked at them in disbelief and thought, "That's what I want to be when I grow up."

Fast forward twenty years and I supported Carrie Bradshaw's decision to pay for shoes over rent in *Sex and the City*. In one episode, she couldn't afford her apartment, but thousands of dollars of Manolos and Jimmy Choos filled her closet and her heart. I coveted Bradshaw's fashion sense, her lack of priority, and her tiny waist. My closet looked nothing like Bradshaw's but I kept aspiring to own more brand-name clothing and to have more options. I never felt like I had enough. Most of the time, I shopped to feel something I wasn't. I rarely bought clothes because I actually needed more clothes. I had plenty. Instead, I purchased clothing to feel a certain way and to be perceived a certain way. While I could never have articulated it then, looking back, it's clear. I wanted to feel smart, beautiful, and loved.

I bought jeans that made me feel skinny, dresses that made me feel sexy, and heels that made me feel powerful. I wore suits to meetings so people would know I belonged in a conference room, even though that's the last place I wanted to be. I shopped for every event and emotion and I still didn't feel better. Something was broken.

Opening my closet was a daily reminder of my bad purchase decisions, weight fluctuation, and of course all the money I had spent. I was living paycheck to paycheck and there were clothes in there I had never even worn. By my mid-thirties, frustrated that nothing I put in my closet had any lasting effect on my happiness or profound meaning in my life, I remembered a saying I had heard once: "I've been shopping my whole life, and I still have nothing to wear." I could relate on so many levels.

If my overflowing closet wasn't a sure sign that it was time to scale back, a trip to Mexico was. On a getaway that lasted less than a week, I brought six pairs of shoes plus the ones I was wearing. I wore flip-flops for the entire trip. Once I started wearing thirty-three items or less, I had more confidence in traveling with fewer items. I went to Europe for a month with just a carry-on bag. I had plenty and was able to focus on discovering new cities instead of wondering if I had enough, or figuring out how to carry around all my stuff.

Remember my big collections of purses and sunglasses? When I pared down to one of each, people were worried about me. They asked me, "What will you do if you lose it, or something breaks?" As if our very survival depends on a well-curated collection of handbags and sunglasses. The answer is simple. If and when I lose something or it breaks, I'll replace it or go without. I refuse to live in fear of not having enough.

I learned so much from dressing with less, but there are five lessons that inspire me to continue to dress with thirty-three items every three months and to recommend it to others:

1. **I need way less than I think to be happy.** The more I had, the more I wanted. It seemed like my clothes needed more clothes. "That sweater would go great with those jeans I have," I would think. Or, "A new scarf or belt will really pull this look together." My constant quest for more resulted in frustration, overspending, and discontent. Choosing from a small selection of thirty-three made me feel light, and I almost immediately felt gratitude for what I had instead of thinking about the next thing I needed.

2. **No one cares what I'm wearing.** What a shock! People weren't thinking about me all the time. All of the efforts to demonstrate who I was by what I wore went unnoticed. When I started the challenge, I was working full time in advertising sales for magazines targeting a very affluent audience. Between in office sales meetings, client lunches, and community events, I was out and about most of the time, with many of the same people. No one noticed I was wearing the same few things for three months. My colleagues didn't notice, my clients didn't notice. I actually received more compliments. I even wore the same dress to every holiday function and event that year.

3. **Deciding what to wear requires mental energy better spent on other things.** Have you ever experienced decision fatigue? Even the cereal aisle at the grocery store is overwhelming with choices. There are fourteen different kinds

of Cheerios. According to *Consumer Reports*, between 1975 and 2008, the number of products in the average supermarket swelled from an average of 9,000 to 47,000. I remember trying on several outfits getting ready in the morning in hopes of finding the perfect thing. Now, in curating a small capsule wardrobe, there are no daily decisions required. I get to wear my favorite things every day.

4. **A simple closet is the gateway to a simple life.** Once you begin to enjoy the benefits of dressing with less, you'll get very curious about living with less. Simplicity in the closet seeps into every other area of your home and life. Once I realized how little I needed in the closet not only to get by but to thrive, I wondered what else was holding me back from even more thriving and happiness. Did I really need all of those spatulas and wire whisks? Why was I holding on to CDs and their cases when my music was all digital?

5. **Simplicity is the way back to love.** It's been my way back to the people I love, work I love, and a life I love. By eliminating everything that doesn't matter, I finally know what does. It's love. (More on how this powerful idea can shape your simplicity journey as it did mine in section four.)

You will never find something that makes you feel beautiful, smart, or loved until you believe you already are. And you are. Simplicity has transformed my heart, my health, and my whole life. I don't spend my evenings poring over sales flyers or my weekends at the mall. I don't covet my neighbor's new car or Carrie Bradshaw's shoe collection. I don't compare what I wear to what you wear and I don't measure my self-worth by my net worth.

Project 333 started as a personal experiment but it turned into a community of people: women, men, moms, artists, corporate people, all kinds of people from around the world who had one thing in common. They finally said enough is enough.

How to Create Your Own Project 333

Imagine what would happen if you invested most of the time, money, and energy you spend on your clothes on the person underneath them. Create a small capsule collection of thirty-three items or less to wear for the next three months. Enjoy a break from closet chaos, and from buying anything new.

THE RULES

- When: Every three months. The official seasons are January–March, April–June, July–September, and October–December. *(It's never too late to start, so join in anytime!)*
- What: Wear only thirty-three items including clothing, accessories, jewelry, outerwear, and shoes. (Yes, shoes too.)
- What not: These items are not counted as part of the thirty-three items—wedding ring or one other sentimental piece of jewelry that you never take off, underwear, sleepwear, in-home loungewear, and workout clothing (your workout clothes have to work out, otherwise they count toward your thirty-three).
- How: Choose your thirty-three items, box up the remainder of your fashion statement, seal it with tape, and put it out of sight.
- What else: Consider that you are creating a wardrobe that you can live, work, and play in for three months. This is not a project in suffering. If your clothes don't fit or are in poor condition, replace them.

How to Clean Out Your Closet for Good

Closet purging and decluttering can be a lifelong battle. Until I started dressing with thirty-three items or less every three months, I cleaned out my closet seasonally. I'd go through my clothes, move things around, take a little out, and add more in. I'd drag storage containers in from the garage, swap out items, try to make a little space, and then go shopping to celebrate a new season. If you search Google for images of a vicious circle, you will likely see me going through the process I just described. When I finally decided to clean out my closet for good, all of these crazy questions and emotions came up.

* Guilt asked, *"Why did you spend so much money on things you don't wear?"*
* Frustration asked, *"Are we going to have to do this again in six months?"*
* Fear asked, *"If you let go, will you have enough?"*

I listened to each question, filled with emotion. After hearing the same questions seasonally for decades, I knew it was time for a change. If your closet decluttering patterns are feeling a little vicious circle-ish, clean out your closet for good. Have fun with this step-by-step guide to cleaning out your closet. This could be the last time you ever have to do it. Once you are finished, you'll be ready for minimalist fashion challenge Project 333.

ROUND ONE

* Put it on your calendar. Depending on the state of your closet, you may need two to five hours or more. Clear the day, hire a sitter, unplug, and make it important.

- Make two playlists: one with your favorite happy, uplifting, everything is going to be okay music and one filled with songs that calm you down. You are going to need good music.
- Bring a water bottle. This is a marathon. You will need water (and snacks).
- Empty your closet. Yes, the whole thing. Completely empty.
- Don't worry about sorting yet, just move everything to your bed. If you put everything on your bed, you'll be motivated to complete the project before bedtime.
- If you have clothes in bureaus, storage containers, or other areas of your home, get those too. Dump them on the bed.
- While you are at it, add your shoes, accessories, and jewelry. All the things.
- Wash your closet. Make it really clean in there. Air it out.
- Take a break. This is a great time to take a walk. Get away from your closet, clothes, guilt, frustration, or any other emotions that are coming up. Walk and breathe. Let go.

ROUND TWO

- Drink water and turn up the music.
- Move the clothes on your bed to piles on the floor with a ruthless first-pass sort. Don't give it too much thought, just go with your first reaction. Sort items into the following piles:
    1. Love: I love these items. They fit me well and I wear them frequently.
    2. Maybe: I want to keep this but I don't know why (you know you have those items).
    3. Donate: These items don't fit my body or my life.
    4. Trash: These items are in poor condition (repurpose if possible).

- Keep going until your bed is clear and you have four piles on the floor.
- Roll around on your bed, kick your feet up in the air and scream, "Almost there!"
- Drink water and eat snacks.
- Box or bag up your items to donate and bring them to your car or garage. Get them out of sight immediately.
- Throw out the trash.
- Take a second pass at your two remaining piles. Try on clothing you aren't sure about and ask the following questions:
    1. Would I go to the store and buy this today?
    2. Will I wear this in the next three to six months (or ever)?
- If the answer is no, start a new donate pile and immediately add it to your other items for donation. Out of sight.

From here, you can either put everything left back in your closet or take the leap and start your own Project 333. Now that you've cleared out the excess, the process of choosing your thirty-three will be much easier. Make a list, by category (clothing, jewelry, accessories, shoes) of the items you know you want to include. Once you have your thirty-three picked out, put them away and get everything else out of sight. You don't have to give away the other stuff, but don't look at it for the next three months. Instead, take the opportunity to enjoy your new smaller wardrobe, and all the space you created. One of the best parts of physically separating myself from my clothes and other things is that my emotional attachment dissipated.

If the idea of dressing with thirty-three items or less is freaking you out a little bit, and you are thinking, "I could never do that!," you aren't alone. When I told my sister about it, she said, "My Project

333 would be thirty-two purses and a pair of jeans." Know that the first reaction most people have is "Not for me"—but then they get curious. This challenge works for men, women, stay-at-home parents, corporate execs, artists, and more. If my version doesn't resonate with you, check out YouTube, search #project333 on Instagram or Google "project 333" and see how different people from around the world are incorporating Project 333 into their closets and lives.

I thought it might be helpful to share some frequently asked questions and answers about the challenge:

Why the number thirty-three? I wish I had a better answer for this, but the truth is, I wanted to create a number that was easy to remember. I thought somewhere between twenty-five and fifty items sounded challenging but achievable for three months, and settled on thirty-three. If thirty-four or fifty-four works better for you, try that. As long as it's challenging, and you are dressing with less, the number isn't that important.

Do your clothes wear out more quickly? My clothes don't wear out more quickly, but I do take better care of them than I did before. I wash all of my clothes in cold water and hang them to dry.

Don't you get bored with your thirty-three items? I don't get bored, but as my wardrobe has become less interesting, my life has become more interesting. If you think you will be bored with a smaller wardrobe, use the challenge as permission to think less about what you wear and more about things you really care about. If you don't know what that is, use the time you aren't spending on your wardrobe figuring it out.

What about special occasions? I include one dress (usually the same one for several seasons) for parties, weddings, or other special occasions.

What if I wear a uniform to work? I suggest counting all of your uniforms as one item in your thirty-three.

What if I need different clothes for work? I started Project 333 while working full time in an office with meetings, events, and lots of people-ing. I had plenty to wear and no one noticed that I was dressing with less. It may help to dress down your work attire just a little bit and dress up your play clothes. Try it and see what does or doesn't work for you.

CHAPTER SIXTEEN

The Upsides of a Downsize

At the beginning stages of planning our downsize, we wondered if we weren't going backward. It was so ingrained in us to believe that success and growth are tied to bigger and better, so a choice to live in a smaller space and live with less brought up some questions. We knew what would make us happy, though, so it really came down to what other people might think and that wasn't going to be a factor in our decision.

It's interesting how we make assumptions about people based on what they own. They have a big house so they must be successful. They have a luxury car so they must be happy. They have boats and jet skis and all the toys so they must have a fun life full of adventure. They wear high-end brands so they must have amazing taste and loads of discretionary income. The 2008 financial crisis brought the truth to light even though we probably already knew it on some level. What you own or don't own doesn't even begin to describe your life. We can't tell if you are successful, happy, adventurous, or what's in your bank account looking from the outside in. You may be trying to tell a story with your stuff, to the outside, or to yourself, but the truth is the truth. I'm sure when I was sitting on a beach in Mexico people thought I had plenty of money, but really I just had a pile of debt. My fancy car with heated seats didn't make me happy. Even buying our first house wasn't everything we thought it would be. We never owned it. The bank did. When we decided to sell after our first Simplicity Summit, we got the same advice from several people who advised that we wait until the market bounced back. They said if we waited ten years, we could make much more on the sale. We considered it, but then we reminded each other that money wasn't going to dictate our decisions anymore. Maybe we'd make more in ten years, and maybe we wouldn't, but that wasn't the issue. We were focused on how we wanted to live for the next ten years. Did we want to take care of a big house? Did we want to replace the roof, the fence, the appliances, the carpet, and all of the other stuff that would likely fall apart over the next ten years? Did we want to continue to invest our money, time, energy, and other resources in a place we didn't really want to live in anymore? Did we want to compromise the next ten years just in case the market bounced back? Our answer was a hard pass.

We started seriously thinking about downsizing after simplifying our lives and decluttering our home. After letting go of so much stuff, we had too much space. In May 2013, we moved from our 2,000-square-foot home to a 750-square-foot apartment. We didn't make a cent on the house sale, but we were finally all the way debt-free. We didn't owe anyone anything. We were free of other things too. Because we made the decision to rent for a while, we were free of the worry of things breaking down. We were free of maintaining a property too. For the first few months in our new space, Mark would wake up on a Saturday, look at me, smile and say, "Guess what I'm not doing this weekend. I'm not (and then he would insert one of the following) raking leaves, shoveling snow, mowing the lawn, or convincing the neighbor to split the cost of a new fence."

I had saved a few boxes of things I didn't know what to do with and wasn't ready to let go of yet. I taped them up and marked them "move to storage and decide later." When we found our new apartment, it didn't come with any storage space. I refused to purchase additional storage space so I let the stuff go. If you offered to pay me a million dollars to tell you what was in those boxes that were so important, I couldn't do it. I don't remember. Real important stuff, right? When we moved into our apartment, it was me, Mark, Bailey, Guinness, and our two cats, Wilbur and Ella. There we were in less than half the space we had in our home, and we had everything we needed. As Francine Jay, author of *The Joy of Less*, suggests, "Your home is a living space, not a storage space."

Since we made the move to a smaller space, we've noticed tremendous upsides to our downsize like less time cleaning, more time to enjoy the outdoors, lower utility bills, no repair or maintenance, and less stress. Here are a few other things we noticed:

1. **Clutter attracts clutter.** When we first moved into our small space, we dedicated a drawer in the kitchen to keep our keys and other things that didn't have a place. Before long, we had a junk drawer filled with odds and ends. Now we hang our keys in the closet and try to find a place for things as they come in, instead of keeping them in a transitional space like a junk drawer.

2. **Less is not nothing.** We are living with much less than we had before, but we still have art on the walls and other

things that we use and appreciate. The goal is not to live with nothing, but to live with things that have meaning and purpose. And that purpose may be to simply enjoy.

3. **You don't have to fill up all the space.** We could have added shelves to the walls and closets or used the space on top of the kitchen cabinets to store or display stuff, but we didn't need to.

4. **Less indoor space provides more time to appreciate the outdoor space.** Since we don't have to clean much or organize, or upgrade and fix stuff, we can appreciate the view of the church across the street, enjoy rooftop views of the mountains, and take hikes overlooking the city.

5. **When you need to buy things for your things, it's time for fewer things.** When we start talking about organizational bins or extra storage options, we know it's time to get rid of stuff instead of accumulating more things to store it in.

6. **Clutter is more obvious.** When you live in a sprawling space, clutter is easier to ignore. In a small space, clutter demands immediate attention.

7. **It's easier to live in the world when you live in a small space.** With less to maintain and worry about, it's easier to work from anywhere, and spend time outside or traveling.

8. **The things that make a place feel like home aren't things.** I had some concerns about making a small apartment feel

like home, but it isn't the things on the walls or the countertop that make a place feel like home. It feels like home when I cook a familiar meal, listen to my favorite music, spend time with my husband and daughter, and when I write.

Before we downsized, there were three of us living in a two-thousand-square-foot home. We had three bedrooms, two bathrooms, an office, a big kitchen and dining room, a family room, and a living room. I never really understood the difference between a living room and a family room except that when I was growing up, we weren't allowed to eat or touch anything in the living room except for special occasions. If all that space wasn't enough, we also had five closets, a big deck, garage, and storage shed in the backyard. Every space was a container for our stuff. We didn't do much entertaining, but because you are supposed to have a table in the kitchen, and the dining room, and on the deck, we had three dining tables. Around those tables were twenty chairs. We had twenty chairs for three people.

People may have thought we were going backward, or making poor financial decisions. The benefits of all of these changes made us less concerned with what other people thought. We just didn't care. The people who loved us still loved us. Downsizing wasn't a step backward for our family. Living with less has given us the time and space to appreciate all of the things that make a house a home. We finally realized that our home is not a container for our stuff. Instead, it is a place for love and connection. We wanted more of that, so we got rid of the stuff and made room for it, room for more love and connection.

CHAPTER SEVENTEEN

The Sound of Letting Go

One morning I woke up in Portland, Oregon, in a cozy Airbnb rental at 5:30 a.m. I like to wake up gently, but that day I was startled awake. It was trash day in the neighborhood I called home for a few nights, and collecting the trash isn't a gentle process. I was in Portland for the Tiny Wardrobe Tour, events in thirty-three different cities to chat about living and dressing with less. I had spent the evening before with a room full of wonderful, thoughtful people. I shared my stories, answered questions, and encouraged everyone to let go. Sometimes I forget that letting go isn't always easy. For some people, attachment isn't an issue. It's easy to let go. For most people, though, myself included, letting go doesn't come naturally. It takes practice and at first it might be painful. The sound of plastic bins being dragged across asphalt that morning in Portland reminded me of the sound that letting go makes.

From the screech and hiss of the air brakes to the giant me-chanical claws wrapping around the bins, to pounds of glass and plastic falling from one container to the next, my eyes flew open. The clattering metal and machinery, humming diesel engine, and whooshing hydraulics filled my ears and mind. The ripping, tearing, and crushing noises reminded me of letting go, but that wasn't the sound of letting go. The scary, jarring noises I heard were the sounds of fear and attachment, the sounds of holding on too tight. Letting go may be hard, but please consider that holding on is harder. You have to hold on every day, and not just to the stuff. You hold on to fear of not having enough, the stress of taking care of everything, and the guilt of spending too much or keeping things you don't use. All the holding on is noisy—deafening sometimes.

As the truck finally pulled away and left me in the early morning silence, I remembered the real sound of letting go: the sound I heard when I started decluttering and letting go, the sound of empty rooms in our house, the sound of walking into our new, smaller space, the sound of becoming debt-free, of waking up stress-free, the sound of being light, and the sound of Monday morning walks instead of Monday morning meetings. That's what letting go sounds like.

The sound of letting go is not the painful, screeching sound I woke up to. Instead, it's the sound of welcoming a new day before the sun comes up, that sound when you can almost hear the stars twinkling.

The calm, the peace, the relief, the joy . . . that's the sound of letting go.

CHAPTER EIGHTEEN

Put Your Hands on Your Heart

I'm so glad we are coming back to our heart practice. In the first section we laid the foundation, and here we will go a little deeper. Instead of focusing on sitting longer, or asking more meaningful questions, prioritize consistency. Come back each day, even if only for a few minutes.

Put Your Hands on Your Heart

I'd like to invite you to join me and develop your own hands-on-heart practice. At the end of each section in the book, I'll ask you to sit quietly and begin to tap into your own soulful simplicity. Engage a little bit each day as you are reading this book and begin to establish your heart practice. If you're ready we can start now, or come back when you are.

Choose a time each day when you can sit alone quietly for a few minutes. While you don't need to do anything special, it may help to light a candle and keep a pen and paper nearby to jot down anything that comes up. Sit on the floor, a chair, your bed, anywhere you feel comfortable, and take a few breaths to settle in and recognize the significance of creating space to listen to your heart.

Try practicing in silence, or with soft music. After a few cleansing breaths in through the nose and out through the mouth, close your eyes, or turn your gaze down and continue focusing on your breath.

Next, place one hand on your heart, and cover your hand with the other. Feel your heart beating. Feel the warmth of your heart and your hands. Now, while continuing to breathe in and out with some intention, and while feeling the warmth, start a conversation with your heart.

Suggested Questions About Making Space

Does this really matter to me? If you are having trouble letting go, ask your heart why. Ask if it matters. Ask what you are really holding on to.

Is this love? If you are considering a new purchase, project, or other commitment, check in first. Will this support love in my life—people I love, work I love, or passions I love? Is this contributing to the life I want, to my health, or to the way I want to treat people? Ask it about your stuff, about how you feel, about your work, about a grudge, about everything. If the answer isn't clear, wait until it is before moving forward.

Do I feel more calm without the clutter? Notice the benefits of making space. Are you feeling less chaos? Is your home feeling more like living space instead of storage space?

What am I making space for? To prevent the need to fill up the empty space you are creating through decluttering, brainstorm better ways to appreciate it.

Put your hands on your heart and ask. Remember, your heart knows things and she will help you make room for what matters most.

MAKING SPACE: ACTION STEPS

Work through this list in any order, trying one thing at a time. This isn't a to-do list or a competition. Consider each action an invitation to learn about letting go and holding on, and to begin making space.

Choose your myth. Take another look at the myths of ownership in chapter 9. Do you see any of your patterns or habits? Once we know why we do what we do, we can make informed choices about how to move forward.

Identify your pain. What is the pain you are numbing? It might be obvious and it might not be, but either way it's worth exploring. Once you know, instead of numbing your pain, you can nurture it and find ways to rise above it.

Take care. Trade your shopping for self-care. Make a list of the things (that aren't things) that lift you up. When you feel like shopping or self-medicating in another way, go to your self-care list first.

Try a purchase pause. Call a stop to shopping for all non-essential items for the next thirty days. Write down everything you want to buy or consider buying and how much each thing costs. At the end of thirty days, add up the money you didn't spend. Ask yourself,

- Is there anything on the list I still want as much as I thought I did?
- If someone handed me the total amount of my fake purchases in cash, would I use it to buy all the things on the list, or use it for something else?

Return it. If you purchased something recently that you don't use, don't enjoy, or feel bad about buying, return it.

Let go of something expensive. What are you holding on to because it's expensive, because you worked so hard for it and paid so much? Let it go. You have paid enough.

Get rid of everything that doesn't matter. Turn on some fun music, grab a box or a bag, and walk around your home filling it with all the stuff you barely notice or don't care about.

Hide it. Have some fun with your family and hide something you are considering getting rid of. Don't tell them it's hidden, but box it up and get it out of sight for sixty days. If no one notices, put it back where it was and let everyone know you are thinking about donating or selling it.

Let the guilt flow. You've attached guilt and other emotions to your stuff, so consider it attached. When the stuff goes, so does the guilt.

Save $1,000. If you don't have an emergency fund yet, start one with $1,000. It will help to navigate the uncertainness of surprises and emergencies with more grace and less stress. Once you are 100 percent debt-free, use Dave Ramsey's advice and baby steps to grow your emergency fund.

Redefine success. Forget about what everyone told you, and even what you may have told yourself about what it means to be successful. Redefine success and rewrite your story.

Surround yourself with simple inspiration. When you are going through big changes like getting rid of stuff and paying down debt, people in your life may not understand or offer the level of support you need. Connect with authors and bloggers sharing their lessons and stories to stay inspired and motivated. See the list of suggested resources at bemorewithless.com/soulful-simplicity-resources.

Share your story. You can be just as inspiring as any of the bloggers or authors who inspire you, or as the people who are encouraging you to change your life. Whether it's sharing your story with a friend over coffee, or by starting a blog, share. Your journey matters.

Host a Simplicity Summit. Follow the recommendations in chapter 14 and arrange a time to sit with your spouse, family members, or yourself and start making a life together. Ask "Wouldn't it be crazy if . . . ?" a lot.

Take me to your closet. Clear a day for a total closet clean-out with the steps in chapter 15 and consider a three-month challenge of wearing thirty-three items or fewer. Share before and after pics of your closet and wardrobe on Instagram with hashtag #project333 and tag me @bemore withless so I can find you and ooh and aah about your progress and bravery.

Consider a smaller space. How would you spend your time if you didn't have so much to take care of? Be open to the upsides of downsizing.

Listen to your heart. Now that you've had a little practice sitting with your hands on your heart, you may be starting to notice little messages during the day. Stay open and keep coming back to your practice.

MAKING TIME:
THE BUSY BOYCOTT

When We Try to Juggle Everything,
We Can't Enjoy Anything

I was that girl—always "so busy" or "crazy busy" or, you know, "good, but busy." I used my busyness as a sign that I was important, needed, and really good at doing it all. I wasn't very good at doing it all, though. I made mistakes, compromised my health, and neglected the people and things in my life that really mattered to me. Being busy became more important than actually getting things done. It was more important than healthy meals, sleep, and presence. I had so much going that it was challenging to stay focused on an entire conversation without thinking about what was on my list of things to do. Before I'd fall asleep each night, I'd mentally run through my list. I could see it on the walls. I can remember many days where my spinning wheels resulted in lots of exhaustion with very little to show for my efforts. Everything changed when I realized I had a choice in how I spent my time and perhaps being lost in busyness wasn't the best use of it. That realization was surprising because I thought I was supposed to be busy. Busyness was part of my definition of success, and I'm not alone.

Wayne Muller, author of *Sabbath*, says, "To be unavailable for our friends and family, to be unable to find time for the sunset (or even know that the sun has set at all), to whiz through our obligations without time for a single, mindful breath, this has become the model of a successful life." I thought I was supposed to run crazy. Looking around, all the people I thought were successful were running crazy too, and the busier they were, the faster they moved, as if they could get more done simply by speeding up. Unfortunately, the rate of speed doesn't result in better quality of work, or even in getting more accomplished. The faster we move, the more mistakes we make, and the more exhausted we become. I used to work in the restaurant industry and I remember in every place I worked, the more customers we had, the faster everyone moved. On the other side, as a customer in restaurants now, I see servers increasing their speed as business picks up, but they aren't getting more done. Instead, they are more forgetful, orders are entered wrong, and in their frenetic state, they are less than attentive to their customers. This is most noticeable in the restaurant and hospitality industry, but it's happening everywhere. After I cleared the clutter and paid off my debt, I had more time and became vigilant about protecting it. I wasn't protecting it to be more productive, or to get more things done. I was protecting it so I could get my life back. After a while, I wasn't saying no because I was so busy, I was saying no because I didn't want to be so busy anymore.

From creating a morning routine to building a business around things I enjoy doing, to lingering instead of rushing, I learned how to make time. It wasn't just saying no and freeing up time, but slowing down the clock by moving through the day with more attention and intention. As I became more aware of how precious my time was, I knew rushing through it wasn't an option anymore. The saying "the days are long, but the years are short" was speaking to me. I decided to stop wishing or wasting time away and start engaging in the moments right in front of me.

If you've ever dreamed about extra hours in the day, or days in the week, or thought about finding time for a sunset, this section about making time will help you make your dreams come true.

CHAPTER NINETEEN

A Meaningful Morning Routine

My morning routine used to look something like this: "snooze button, snooze button, snooze button, oh no, I'm running late, coffee, shower, kid in car, start the day half asleep running late and frantic." It was less of a routine and more of a bad habit. Once I started taking yoga classes, I wanted to experience what I felt when I left class even on the days I didn't have a class so I started a tiny practice of my own each morning. It was about five minutes of yoga, but even that gave me a little boost. When we got serious about paying off our debt, I remember scoffing at Dave Ramsey's advice to save $1,000 for an emergency fund before paying down debt faster. Focusing on behavior instead of math worked. If you are skeptical about adding more things to your already busy day to make more time, stay focused on the behavior. It will make a difference. Spending time first thing each day on a meaningful morning routine will help you make more time throughout the day. It sounds counterintuitive, but it works.

My morning routine started when I decided to trade one of my snoozes for five minutes alone on my yoga mat practicing what I had learned in class. It was all I had time for at first. Those five minutes made such a difference in how I approached my day, so I decided to add another five minutes. Next, instead of extending my yoga practice past ten minutes, I added five minutes of writing, and then five minutes of meditation. After a few weeks, I traded all of my extra snooze buttons for a thirty-minute practice of writing, yoga, and meditation each morning. That became my meaningful morning routine. The rest of my day was still chaotic, but those thirty minutes helped me handle the chaos a little better. My morning routine became a place I could revisit during the day instead of overreacting or getting anxious about everything I had on my plate. I had more energy, more intention, and more presence. Not only that, but I started looking forward to those thirty minutes each morning. Before I checked e-mail, made my daughter breakfast, or had to answer to anyone else, I fed myself first.

Habit Stacking

If you'd like to create a meaningful morning routine, I recommend using habit stacking. Build your routine slowly, habit by habit and minute by minute. You probably already practice habit stacking without even knowing it. If you wake up, take a shower, use shampoo, then conditioner, dry off, and get dressed, you're a stacker. Perhaps you stack in the evening by brushing your teeth, washing your face, and reading a book before bed. You can probably identify little pockets of habit stacks throughout your day. While I strongly believe in the power of building habits one at a time, habit stacking gives you the momentum to build multiple habits simultaneously. Each habit triggers and supports the one to follow.

Think about your morning routine as a little stack of habits. Start with one, and build slowly. If you are an all-or-nothing kind of person when it comes to habits, this will be challenging, but try to stick with the slow build. I used to jump right in when it came to habit changes, but it wasn't until I took a slower, more intentional approach that my habits began to stick. Much of my slow-habit in-spiration comes from Leo Babauta, founder of the *Zen Habits* blog. He advocates slow and steady change. Here's an example he shared for people who wanted to start a flossing habit: "Start your habit by just flossing one tooth. It's so remarkably easy that you won't be able to say it's too hard, or you don't have the time. It will feel a bit ridic-ulous but just do it. On day two, floss two teeth. Slowly expand every one to three days until you're flossing all your teeth. Sure, you won't get the full benefit of flossing all your teeth at first, but the key is not to get the full benefit but to create a habit that lasts."

Use one of these seven-week, slow-build, habit-stacking plans to create your morning routine.

TWO-ACTIVITY PLAN:

Week One:

2 Activities for 5 minutes each. Total: 10 minutes.

Week Two:

2 Activities for 6 minutes each. Total: 12 minutes.

Week Three:

2 Activities for 7 minutes each. Total: 14 minutes.

Week Four:

2 Activities for 8 minutes each. Total: 16 minutes.

Week Five:

2 Activities for 10 minutes each. Total: 20 minutes.

Week Six:

2 Activities for 12 minutes each. Total: 24 minutes.

Week Seven:

2 Activities for 15 minutes each. Total: 30 minutes.

THREE-ACTIVITY PLAN:

Week One:

2 Activities for 5 minutes each. Total: 10 minutes.

Week Two:

3 Activities for 5 minutes each. Total: 15 minutes.

Week Three:

3 Activities for 6 minutes each. Total: 18 minutes.

Week Four:

3 Activities for 7 minutes each. Total: 21 minutes.

Week Five:

3 Activities for 8 minutes each. Total: 24 minutes.

Week Six:

3 Activities for 9 minutes each. Total: 27 minutes.

Week Seven:

3 Activities for 10 minutes each. Total: 30 minutes.

A slow build helps you ease in and makes your new routine sustainable. As you free up more time in your life, you may want to extend your morning routine. Now that I have more flexibility, my morning routine can last up to three hours. I change it seasonally and may include a combination of yoga, writing, walking, meditation, reading, and my hands-on-heart practice. Your goal is not to be the best morning routine maker ever, but instead to engage in activities that fuel you and to notice boosts in health, happiness, kindness, and inspiration. Enjoy your life through the intention and purpose you are creating habit by habit, day by day, and minute by minute.

You May Run into Roadblocks Along the Way

Most of us with good intentions and new habits face resistance, distraction, and unexpected roadblocks. This is part of the habit-building process. Each time something comes up and derails your habit, you make a choice to throw in the towel or start over and try again. That intentional choice defines you and future decisions too. It's not the action, but your reaction, that sets the stage. Here are a few roadblocks that may come up with recommendations to move through them:

1. **You hit the snooze button instead of getting up early.**
   While doing your morning routine first is important, if

occasionally you have to do it later in the day, do it. Don't use getting up late as an excuse to completely miss your daily stack of habits.

2. **You are sick and don't feel like practicing your morning routine.** If you miss one day, get back on track the next day as if nothing happened. If you miss a few days in the first two weeks, start over. Build your practice from the beginning. It may also help to think through your morning routine even if you aren't actually practicing it. According to AsapScience, "From a neuro-scientific standpoint, imagining an action and doing it requires the same motor and sensory programs in the brain. Because imagination and action are actually integrated and engage the same neuro pathways practicing one actually influences the others." They share a study where two groups practiced piano for two hours a day, but one of those groups only practiced mentally. They didn't have pianos. Both groups experienced similar changes in the brain, and even more surprising was that after three days, both groups demonstrated the same amount of accuracy in playing. Instead of abandoning your morning routine completely, go through the motions in your mind while you are nursing your illness.

3. **Your child stays home from school, or you have an early appointment.** Instead of skipping your routine altogether, practice a shorter version. Go to the space where you practice and acknowledge the space and importance of the practice. Even that simple step will keep you on track and connected to your morning routine.

4. **You are traveling.** When you are traveling, you might have to adjust to new schedules and spaces. Think of it as an adventure to recreate your morning routine wherever you are. You'll have to find new spaces to practice and stay open to switching up the activities you include if you need something different for fuel while on the road. It helps to make the space and time if you can, even if your practice is shorter than or a different combination from your usual stack of habits.

5. **You can't find a quiet space.** If you struggle to find a place to practice your morning routine because your family is there, ask them for help. Tell them about your morning routine and why it's important to you and ask for the time and space you need. Let them know you'll be a better wife/husband/mom/dad/friend/human if you can practice your meaningful morning routine. You may even inspire your loved ones to start a morning routine of their own.

6. **You have a crazy-busy day ahead.** Even though I know how powerful my morning routine is, there are times I skip it because of the demands of the day. Each time I do that and jump into work or other obligations first, I'm not as focused, creative, productive, or loving as I am when I take a few minutes to be mindful. It always pays off to start with your morning routine. You'll feel less anxious and more focused if you start with what you need most.

Approach Your New Routines and Habits with Joyful Discipline

The word *discipline* sometimes has a negative connotation, but once you experience the benefits of your morning routine or other healthy habits, you'll find the joy in discipline and begin to think of it as a gift instead of a punishment. If you struggle with creating or sticking with your morning routine, approach it with joyful discipline instead of a feeling of boredom or sacrifice.

These recommendations will help you create joyful discipline:

1. **Choose wisely**

   Create your routine with a mix of habits and activities that contribute to long-term health and good work, but also offer immediate benefits. For instance, drinking green smoothies helps you consume more fruits and veggies, but adding ginger gives you a daily zing that will result in early morning smiles.

2. **Adjust for inflation**

   If your schedule blows up with something unexpected, without joyful discipline, you might feel resentful or frustrated. Plan to be surprised, and let go when you need to.

3. **Adjust for deflation**

   You may have created your routine for days when you are full of energy and focus. If you toss and turn the night before, you might not have the level of commitment you have after an eight-hour snooze. Instead of pushing through, adjust, back off, and do less.

4. Pivot

Pay attention to how your routine is treating you. Do you feel healthier, happier, and more loving, or stressed and run-down? If after some time, your routine is not contributing to your well-being so you can contribute at a higher level to everyone around you, change things up.

5. Protect

Even though you will be adjusting for inflation and deflation, it's up to you to protect your routine by saying no, changing your schedule, and giving yourself the space you need to grow, thrive, and heal.

6. Smile

If your routine includes an early morning trip to the gym, and you scowl as you turn off your alarm clock at five a.m., commit to smiling when you wake up. Stretch and smile before you get out of bed. Instead of thinking about how much you want to sleep in, remember how fortunate you are to have the opportunity to get up and work out. It might be a hard sell at first, but after a few days, your smile will begin to change your attitude.

7. Collaborate

Include other people in your routine. As someone who loves to spend time quietly creating, I know how hard this can be. Schedule calls with people who lift you up or invite friends for a weekly walk. Even if you work with other people all day long, intentionally including the right people in your routine can make a big difference.

8. Rotate

If boredom is something you worry about, have two or three routines that you rotate throughout the week.

9. Unroutine

Schedule one day a week to wake up with no plans or obligations. This might be a good day to unplug your computer, take your Fitbit off, and remember what it's like to let the day unfold.

10. Remember your why

When you create your routine, write a few sentences about why you want to structure your day with intention. When you are feeling unmotivated to continue, read what you wrote down for inspiration to practice even when you don't feel like it.

CHAPTER TWENTY

1:11

I read about a working mom who organized her time so ruthlessly that she always keyed in 1:11 or 2:22 or 3:33 on the microwave rather than 1:00, 2:00, or 3:00, because she realized hitting the same number three times took less time. There is no doubt in my mind that this working mom had a full plate. Too full. But how much time was she gaining? Instead of squeezing seconds out of a microwaved lunch, removing a nonessential item from her to-do list or asking for help on a project would have provided more relief. When we focus more on fitting it all in instead of making time for what counts, we lose sight of how to create a meaningful life. Instead of fully experiencing the gift in front of us, we cram our days and lives with all the things. And juggling everything makes it impossible to enjoy anything.

Ten years ago, I would have tried to implement this strategy of 1:11 because I too was determined to fit it all in. Instead of doing less, I'd turn to a productivity hack that I thought would allow me to do more. Like making ends meet, it became a bad habit. I kept saying yes, kept piling it on, and kept falling behind. I measured who I was by what I got done. If you've ever used your to-do list or calendar as a report card to assess your self-worth, you know what I mean. I remember many evenings comparing list to list at the end of the day with my husband. "How was your day?" he'd ask. And I'd say something like, "Busy day, I did a, b, c, d," listing my many accomplishments. If his list was longer, I'd remember I had forgotten to mention a few things on my list and add more. There was always more.

If our to-do lists don't have enough check marks and inbox zero is still miles away, we feel like we didn't contribute enough and therefore we aren't good enough. I have to remind myself that no one cares about what's on my to-do list or how busy I am, or even how much I got done yesterday. What I do is not who I am.

When Your Plate Is Full, You Have Three Choices

1. Worry about everything on your plate, and complain about how crazy busy you are. Keep piling on more and more until you burn out, break down, or somehow finally get through it all and then burn out and break down.

2. Remove something from your plate to make room for something that matters more.

3. Recognize your plate is full and say no to everything else so you can enjoy and engage in what is right in front of you.

Real connection doesn't come from comparing our lists or our plates, it comes from sharing our hearts. Instead of measuring ourselves by what we get done, let's measure by how we treat people and how we engage in our work. Let's measure more by what's in our hearts, and less by what's on our lists.

CHAPTER TWENTY-ONE

The Busy Boycott

As the regional advertising director for a group of luxury magazines, I thought it was my job to be on all the time. I checked my e-mail constantly. My phone was always on, and I would respond to clients and colleagues within minutes or seconds. Even that wasn't enough. I wanted to do it better, faster, more. There was a time in my hurried, must-get-it-all-done life when I looked into getting an office set up in my car. I wanted a laptop hooked up to the dash like police officers have. I thought it would be so much more efficient to e-mail at stoplights from a laptop instead of a phone. Better, faster, more.

An Ordinary Morning

I could tell the light was flooding the room before I opened my eyes. I rolled over and stretched with my eyes still closed. I smiled thinking about the day ahead. I had no plans or obligations. It was just after six a.m. on a summer morning and the day was all mine. I thought about how I could embrace the light and the time and space I created and how I could savor the early morning moments. I woke up slowly, got out of bed, brushed my teeth and drank a glass of water. I curled up with my notebook and wrote a few pages of words and thoughts that had built up from the day before and settled in my brain overnight, like scar tissue. Writing it down helped me to break it up and let go of the ideas and emotions that were holding on and busying my mind. When I was finished writing, I sat quietly in meditation for fifteen minutes, drank a hot cup of tea and went for a long walk in the sunshine. This wasn't a calorie-burning walk. I stopped frequently to notice and appreciate beautiful things and new views. Once, I even stopped to close my eyes and look up to the sun. Feeling the warmth of the sun on my face, I said a silent prayer: "Fill me with light and grace. Energize me. Love me."

Sounds like a good morning, right? If you are nodding your head yes right now, thank you. You are very kind and a better person than I used to be. If you had told me a few years ago that you spent your morning praying in the sunshine while I was in the throes of my busy addiction, I would have quickly rolled my eyes and thought, "Lady, get a job." I would have pretended I was annoyed, but what I would have been feeling was jealousy. I was too busy for the easy mornings I craved. Instead, I used to wake up, coffee up, rush my daughter out the door, and get to work. I complained about my busyness and got completely high from it at the same time. I was a busy addict.

I started rethinking my busy addiction one afternoon after a crazy day at work. I was driving my daughter home from school. I was barreling down the freeway with my phone to my ear, and she was telling me about her day. This is hard for me to admit, but she was used to talking to me while I was doing other things. I knew she was talking to me and I wanted to be as engaged as I could so I was nodding, glancing over at her, and even responding occasionally with one- or two-word sentences. It was all I could do as I was busy getting back to clients and crunching numbers on my phone . . . and driving.

When we got home, I pulled into the garage and watched her get out of the car and slowly walk to the door with her backpack. It struck me that I could barely remember any of our conversation, let alone the drive home. I was so consumed with being busy that I risked our lives driving as distracted as I was and missed a precious opportunity to connect with my child. I wanted to give her more, but I wasn't even giving her my attention. Tears pooled in my eyes when I thought of all the afternoons, all the phone calls, and all of the missed moments.

When I thought about it, I realized that picking my daughter up from school was completely different from really being there for her. It wasn't just in the car either. My phone was like a body part. It was always nearby, and it came first. I thought I was so busy because the job demanded it, and because life demanded it, and because everyone wanted more from me. I didn't know it was my choice. I didn't realize this was the life I was choosing; the life I was creating. In an interview with *The Washington Post*, Brené Brown said, "The expectations of what we can get done, and how well we can do it, are beyond human scale." My focus was on getting it all done instead of getting anything done well.

The day after our afternoon drive home, I thought about how I ignored my daughter in favor of my phone. I vowed not to miss another opportunity for connection, and banned my phone from the car. I decided I was going to show all the way up for the people I love, starting with her. That's the day I unknowingly began my busy boycott. And can you guess what happened? My clients didn't notice. My boss didn't notice. My sales went up, and most important, my daughter came first, not just in my thoughts but through my actions too.

The Busy Boycott—a Twenty-one-day Challenge to Help You Slow Down

Busyness has become more pervasive than clutter in complicating our lives. We have plenty of decluttering strategies, but what should we do about our busy lives? I'd like to suggest a busy boycott. You might not think you have time for a revolution right now, but if you ever want time for a life that matters, this is the right time to revolt.

Try the following twenty-one-day challenge and practice each of these three simple steps for seven days each.

1. **Stop talking about it. (Days one–seven)**

   For all that is good and holy, let's stop telling each other how busy we are. Perhaps, if we can physically remove the word *busy* from the conversation, we can stop thinking about it so much. When you tell someone how busy you are, you remind yourself too. You might feel busier than you actually are. Not only that, but often "I'm so busy" comes across as "I'm too busy for you."

   For the next seven days, ban the word *busy* from your vocabulary. This may be more challenging than you think. When you catch yourself mid-sentence using the word *busy*, use it as an opportunity to change your response and the conversation.

   Tip: Avoid hearing the word *busy* by asking better questions. Instead of "How are you?" try "What made you smile today?" My daughter often asks, "Did anything interesting happen today?" By changing the questions and conversation, you open up space for connection.

2. Do less. (Days eight–fourteen)

Instead of searching for more efficient ways to do it all, do less. Say no, and protect your time for what matters most to you. Work with people who want your best, not your busiest. Stop comparing your lists, your life, and your love. Every day for the next seven days, eliminate one thing from your calendar or to-do list. Don't postpone it, let it go. If you are really worried about missing something, write it down and put it in an envelope. If you don't miss it or even remember it at the end of the week, toss the envelope.

Tip: Know your strengths. What do you do best? What can you delegate or release completely?

3. Linger longer. (Days fifteen–twenty-one)

A busy life says, "Hurry up! You're falling behind. Do more!" A slow one says, "You can stop now. It's okay to be still and listen to your soul or stop to say a prayer in the warmth of the sunshine." There is no guilt in self-care, and no shame in lingering or waking up slowly.

Slowing down supports your commitment to create and protect your newfound time and space. Savor good food, conversation, and beautiful views. Fall in love. Smile. Breathe. Then, fall in love again.

Tip: Lose the guilt. Instead of thinking about the opposite of busyness as laziness, consider that the opposite of a busy life is a full, intentional life.

If busyness has compromised your health, relationships, or work or if it has silenced your soul, take action with a busy boycott. With more demands on our time, the advances in modern-day technology, and our desire to be seen, accomplished, and important, the pressure is on to do more with less. Instead, join me, boycott busy and be more with less.

CHAPTER TWENTY-TWO

Creating Soul-Centered Work

Every job I had eventually ran me into the ground. When my daughter was born, I was living the American dream so I took a full six weeks off. As if forty-two days are enough to become a mother. I remember many of those forty-two days staying home with my little girl and wishing the hours would pass more slowly so I could hold her longer, smell the back of her neck for a few more minutes, and watch her grow a little while longer. When I went back to work and dropped her off at day care, I thought back to the fears I had before she was born. Would I remember what my baby looked like at the end of the day? Could I pick her out in the sea of day care babies? At work, I felt like a bad mom, and at home, I felt like I was going to lose my job for being distracted with my new baby. I remember running into the bathroom at work pumping milk, embarrassed that my colleagues might hear. Then, I'd rush over to the day care center to feed my baby on my lunch break. What was I thinking? It was too much, so I switched her to formula. A few days later, she broke out in hives with a milk allergy. I was almost re-lieved. Now feeding her came first. I could put her before my work without feeling guilty or judged. Note: no one was judging, but I was so tired and overwhelmed I imagined they were.

When Bailey was two and I began to care for her by myself as a single mom, I wanted her day care days to end. I wanted to be there for her. So I worked harder with the intention of making more money now to have more flexibility later. The *more + more = more* equation failed me again. I was missing her life. Mornings and evenings were not enough. Years later, after Mark, Bailey, and I moved to Utah, I took another soul-sucking job, but not without the promise of working some afternoons at home. I wanted to pick my girl up from school and be with her for a little bit longer each day. It was a step in the right direction, but bringing my work home still stole my attention.

When I was diagnosed with MS, I didn't think I would even-tually quit my job. In fact, to prove to everyone I was okay, I dug my heels in a little deeper at first. I was worried about potential medical bills, long-term disability, and again, what other people might think, so I made sure work was a priority—stepping outside of myself to prove my worth again. As Mark and I paid off our debt, focused on fewer ends, got rid of our stuff, and began to reject the idea that what other people thought about our life mat-tered or should influence our decisions, I started to consider the idea of working for myself. I knew I didn't want to be tied down to an office space or local business, and I wondered if sharing my simplicity journey through a blog could be the start of something. I wasn't sure, but I was excited to try it anyway. In May 2010, bemorewithless.com was born. I even registered my business as a way to say to myself, "I am doing this. This is possible." I was still working full time, but doing something I really cared about made the work I didn't love a little more bearable.

Instead of Becoming Your Work, Choose Work That Becomes You

When I think about why my jobs always wore me down, I can't entirely blame the jobs. Some of my employers were great, I loved my clients, and some of the work was enjoyable. The real problem was me. I became my work instead of choosing work that becomes me. I used to think I was an extrovert. People who know me well laugh about that. My former boss and wonderful friend Diana saw it. She thrived at big events and client lunches while I used to try to leave early whenever I could. I showed up, though, and pretended I liked it and because I was good at it, most people didn't know how miserable I was. The work I did was very high energy and demanded constant interaction with lots of other people. I became the person I thought I was supposed to be to do my job. I was what author Glennon Doyle would describe as *shiny*. She says, "You can either be shiny and admired or real and loved." Being shiny means not being you. Shiny doesn't last, or feel good, or matter. Loved is always the better bet. When I was working, I was shiny. I remember one of my shiniest moments when Mark and I were attending an event at one of my clients' photography studios. I knew it would be a schmoozefest and wasn't looking forward to it. In the car on the way over, I wasn't very talkative. I was exhausted and not feeling well and took it out on Mark with short answers, sarcasm, and feeling sorry for myself. When we walked through the door of the studio, I turned on my shiny work-self and was hugging and mingling and appearing to have a great time. When we left, Mark was hurt and confused. "What just happened? I thought you didn't feel well," he said. I responded, "I have to *show up* for work." We never talked about it again, but I'm sure he was thinking, "I'd like you to show up for me."

Now that I know I'm an introvert, it seems more obvious why my work wore me down, why I got sick a bunch, why I dreaded the obligatory networking events, and why I felt completely depleted at the end of every workday, meeting, or event. I never took the time to be alone, to refuel, or to soothe my heart. Instead, I kept pushing, proving, and trying to thrive. There was always more to be done, more to prove, bigger goals, and higher hoops.

Books like *Quiet: The Power of Introverts in a World That Can't Stop Talking* by Susan Cain encourage introverts to be who they are. It's in that place where we are who our hearts want us to be that we can be all the way alive. Becoming my work and acting like an extrovert for a really long time was part of stepping outside of myself and forgetting who I was. I lost myself. I forgot who I was and what I needed to thrive. I didn't need a personality test to tell me I was an introvert. I needed some space and breathing room to remember. I had to say, "enough is enough." I had to be still and listen.

Growing My Soul-Centered Business

I started working on the blog in April 2010 and published my first post that May. It was the first of many small steps in creating a soul-centered business that has evolved in the most surprising ways. I didn't know much in the beginning, but I did know I wanted to encourage people to simplify their lives for better health and more love in their lives. The stress from the work I was doing at my day job was overwhelming—partly because of the corporate culture, but mostly because after several years of simplifying my life, I didn't believe in the work I was doing anymore. I wanted to create work that supported better health and more love in my own life including flexible hours, the opportunity to be creative, and a revenue model that allowed me to reject advertising pitches and other requests that weren't aligned with my heart and soul.

I was still working full time at my soul-sucking job when I started, but from the moment I pressed "publish" on my first post, again I could feel the weight lifting. Sixteen months later, I gave my notice and became a full-time creative entrepreneur. Forgoing a steady paycheck was scary, but I knew it was worth it the first time I got to wake up and take Guinness for a walk around the lake instead of going to another Monday morning weekly meeting. Recently, someone asked me what my favorite part of my business is and I said writing, but after giving it some thought, I realized that the best part of my work is that it is soul-centered. What I mean by that is I trust myself to know what's best for my business. I don't ignore what I know to be true in the name of making more money, growing faster, or pleasing someone else. It's not always easy, but it's the simplest, most rewarding way to do business. It means I don't say yes when my heart says no.

A soul-centered business gives me the confidence to try things when I don't know if they will work, the clarity to know the difference between helpful criticism and negative feedback, and the strength to know when to let go. Working from a soul-centered place allows me to notice when I'm working too much, or working in a way that isn't supporting health and love in my life. When that's happening I can change course quickly instead of waiting for a breakdown.

If I put my heart and soul on the line word after word, post after post, and day after day, I will connect with people who connect with the real me. We are alike. We are like-hearted. Instead of buying attention with advertising, I stay focused on offering helpful solutions, sharing my story, and appreciating every moment of the connection I share with people who visit my site, take a course, or read this book because I know how important it is to my work, my heart, and my soul. Like a soulful simplicity, creating a soul-centered business involves quietly and consistently noticing what matters most to me, and figuring out how to keep those most important things front and center.

CHAPTER TWENTY-THREE

A Gentle Warrior's Manifesto to End Busyness

Once I began to identify what mattered to me and was doing what was necessary to protect it, I moved from frantic victim of busyness to gentle warrior. My tactics were fierce but also soft in defending my time from a society that always wants more. To protect and defend, you sometimes have to draw a line in the sand. What I've learned, though, is that if you can draw the line with your heart, you can take a stand with a smile, dump the guilt around doing less, and instead of disappointing others, remind them what's important in their own lives by honoring what's important in yours.

My manifesto is a list of my nonnegotiables that guide me, especially when I struggle with the call to do more.

A Gentle Warrior's Manifesto to End Busyness

1. **I will not say yes when my heart says no.**

   Most of the time, when presented with an opportunity or invitation, I know the answer. My heart knows long before I take the time to consider what I'll say. When I think about saying yes when my heart says no, I can feel the conflict in my body. I might clench my teeth, squeeze my hands, or feel stress where there should only be light. For many years, I ignored those outside signs of inside struggle, but now I pay attention.

   Be a gentle warrior.

   Protect what matters and say no with a kind smile. Instead of saying yes when your heart says no, be honest. Your no doesn't need a lengthy explanation or apology. Saying no more honestly will give you a chance to say yes to who and what you genuinely care about. (See more on how to say no in chapter 26.)

2. **I will measure more by what's in my heart and less by what's on my list.**

   If there weren't enough items crossed off my to-do list or I didn't do more than everyone around me, I felt like a failure. If I was home sick and couldn't contribute at all, I'd feel even worse about myself. I thought if I could do more, perform better, and climb the ladder faster, I'd be happier, more successful, and people would love me more. As I slowly pulled back and started thinking about how I really wanted to spend my time, I realized people couldn't love me for what I accomplished, but only for who I really was. When I was consumed with doing more, I didn't even know who I really was.

Be a gentle warrior.

Measure more by what's in your heart and by how you treat people, including yourself. If you notice you are feeling down because of the things you left undone, remind yourself who you are and what you mean to the people around you.

3. I will prioritize love and health.

Love and health matter to me, but until I became a gentle warrior and began to protect them, respect them, and create an environment where they could thrive, love and health never had a chance to rise up. I experienced love and health in my life before, but not like I do now. I used to catch glimpses of both, but today my life is full of love and health.

Be a gentle warrior.

Know what matters most to you, and when you are making a decision ask yourself what will support the things that matter most to you. Let your priorities guide you.

4. I will ask for help.

I can get by alone, but getting by is not what I want for my life. When I ask for help and bring other people in, everything is elevated. Last summer, when a friend helped me thrive in my work and I thanked him, he replied, "When you rise, I smile." That statement reminded me that asking for help doesn't help just me, but everyone around me. We are all in this together.

Be a gentle warrior.

Asking for help is not weakness, but a sign of strength. Asking for help builds relationships. Even though you *can* do it alone, you can do it better with help every time.

5. I will work with people who want my best, not my busiest.

I used to spend every Monday morning in meetings with no meaning. I used to spend hours writing weekly reports because people I worked with needed proof I was busy. Now that I work for myself, I decide how I spend my time, how I grow my business, and who I work with.

Be a gentle warrior.

If you work for someone who prioritizes busy work over good work, make subtle shifts if you aren't in a position to make a big change. Suggest standing meetings, or agendas that support a team. Challenge your coworkers to check e-mail only a few times a day and to turn off chat or notifications during certain times of the day. Go for walks during your lunch hour instead of eating at your desk. Recognize and demonstrate that busyness is not productivity, creativity, or love. Work with people who want your best work, not your busy work.

If you are the one requesting the meetings and reports, make sure they have a purpose. Trust the people who work for you and encourage their best work, not their busy work.

6. I will ask better questions so we don't have to talk about how busy we are.

Let's stop telling each other how busy we are. That conversation isn't helping us connect, or become less busy.

Talking about busyness makes me feel busy, even when I'm not. Instead of "How are you?" I am going to ask people, "What was the best part of your day?" or "Who or what made you smile today?" or "What will you remember about this week?"

Be a gentle warrior.

Ban the word *busy* and see what it feels like to talk about your life differently. "I'm so busy" is usually a complaint. You roll your eyes, shrug your shoulders, and often sigh when rambling about your busy day. Instead, talk about your day with gratitude. Focus your conversations on the things you are grateful for and see how that changes things. Go deeper with the busy boycott challenge in chapter 21.

7. **I will not let my phone run my life.**

Phones were designed for connection, but the more our phones can do, the less connected we seem to be. I used to use my phone everywhere, checking it constantly, even in the car.

Be a gentle warrior.

Turn off all notifications on your phone. Do you really need to know when you get a new e-mail or Facebook message? Silence your phone when you are in the car, sharing a meal, sleeping, or doing other things that benefit from your undivided attention. Experiment with phone-free days, and removing social media apps and e-mail from your phone.

8. **I will trade my FOMO for JOMO.**

By committing to do less, I am going to miss out on things, but instead of fear, I feel joy. Joy that I have a choice, joy that I am protecting what matters most, and joy because I feel well. Because I am doing less, I get to choose the things that mean the most, and I have the attention and energy to be engaged and truly enjoy what I'm doing.

Be a gentle warrior.

FOMO—fear of missing out—signals a lack of engagement. If you are worried about what you are missing, you aren't connecting with the most meaningful parts of what's happening right now. Letting go of FOMO means abandoning the need to catch up, keep up, and measure up to connect with what's right in front of you. Don't be surprised if you actually look forward to missing the things that you used to do because you felt obligated, or fearful of missing out. Trade your FOMO (fear of missing out) for JOMO (joy of missing out).

9. I will create space for solitude.

If I need to decline an invitation to spend time alone, I will. If necessary, I'll reschedule or cancel thoughtfully without explanation. I enjoy spending time with people I love and engaging in fun activities, but as an introvert, I need time alone. Without solitude, I feel depleted. Without quiet, I become overwhelmed and grouchy.

Be a gentle warrior.

Introverts need solitude, but so do extroverts. Protect your soul's need for silence and retreat. Take the time you need to retreat, refuel, and then go back into the world with a full heart.

10. I will linger longer.

I will watch sunrises and sunsets. I will slow down and taste my food. I will let moments move me to laughter or to tears. I will take time to notice love in the details and joy in someone's eyes. I'll create space to nurture creative work knowing that I can't schedule a good idea, plan when words will flow, or orchestrate the magic of everything coming together just the way it was always meant to.

Be a gentle warrior.

Don't apologize for daydreaming, stargazing, or any activity that speaks to your soul. Take a long walk, a short nap, or sit quietly. Others may not respect the value of slowing down, but you know what's best for you.

Become a Gentle Warrior and Protect What Matters Most to You

Cherish and protect your health, your love, your loves, and your life by making a list of your own nonnegotiables. Do this with the heart of a gentle warrior and your efforts won't be selfish or isolating, but instead will allow you to be and give your best self. These nonnegotiables or life rules won't limit you. Creating boundaries makes room to expand in all directions.

CHAPTER TWENTY-FOUR

Sabbath

The fruitful uselessness of rest, play, and delight can begin on a Sabbath morning. Wake up, but do not get up. Do something delightful. Use your imagination, be frivolous, be daring. Invent rituals. Do nothing of significance.

—WAYNE MULLER

We are weary because we do not rest. Weekends have become more about catching up, running errands, and planning for the next week than about resting or enjoying the day. You probably do one or more of the following on your day off: grocery shopping, banking, cleaning, laundry, washing the car, entertaining, catching up on work, catching up on TV, catching up on e-mail, and catching up on catching up. Some of those things are productive, fun, and even necessary, but when do your body, mind, and soul get to rest? The one time we actually take a day off is when we are sick. And why are we sick? Because we are weary. Our bodies will eventually force rest, but we pay the price inside and out by refusing to be proactive.

Wayne Muller, the author of *Sabbath*, points out that while Sabbath may be a holy day for some, it can be anything that provides "a visceral experience of life-giving nourishment and rest." When was the last time you experienced life-giving nourishment and rest? He suggests that Sabbath time can be a refuge from our modern life, which is designed to seduce our attention. Muller lists the distractions attempting to seduce us, such as hundreds of channels of television, e-mail, magazines, and billboards, and I'd add a few things to that list like Facebook, Twitter, Pinterest, and other social media platforms. I never practiced the Sabbath growing up as an Episcopalian, but I've long admired the tradition and ritual.

I like the idea of a day for rest, but that wasn't always the case. On a visit to Copenhagen many years ago, I was disappointed that much of the city was closed down on Sunday. On the last day of my trip, I went back to a boutique to buy a pair of boots I had tried on a few days before. I was devastated that my boots were behind a locked door. While I could have been experiencing life-giving nourishment and rest, I had my nose pressed to a closed store window, moaning, "No, no, this can't be happening, maybe they open at noon."

Fast forward several years and several pairs of subpar boots, and what I want more than anything is the Sabbath that Muller describes. If you want that too, then follow these simple instructions.

HOW TO CREATE YOUR OWN SABBATH

1. **Schedule your Sabbath.** Put it on your calendar and make it important.

2. **Tell the world.** Call your friends, text your colleagues, tweet the news that you have scheduled a day off and won't be available. Let them know you won't be answering the phone, checking e-mail, or updating your Facebook status.

3. **Take a Sabbath eve.** On the night before your planned day off, skip the heavy meal and alcohol. Go to bed early so you can wake up feeling peaceful and refreshed.

4. **Make a Sabbath box.** This was a lovely suggestion from *Sabbath*. Put anything in the box that you don't want to use during your day off. Include your phone, tablets, and other digital devices. Mentally place things in the box that won't fit, like your washing machine, car, and other things that invite you into chores and busyness. Also include things left undone, and worries, by writing them on a piece of paper and placing it in the box.

5. **Time-out.** When I go on vacation, the thing I love most is not being aware of what time it is and not caring. If you can afford this luxury, turn off your clocks and don't worry about what time it is. Eat when you're hungry, drink when you're thirsty, and sleep when you're tired.

6. **Leave the "shoulds" in the Sabbath box.** If you are really going to take a day off, don't worry about what you should or should not be doing. If you want to take three naps, take three naps. Lunch in bed? Why not?

7. **Make a promise to yourself** that you won't spend the day after making up for your day off.

Digital Sabbaticals

When author Tammy Strobel was writing *You Can Buy Happiness and It's Cheap*, she took a monthlong digital sabbatical. She said, "The Internet brings me an incredible amount of happiness. I love connecting with readers, writers, and keeping up with friends and family. But if I spend too much time online, I start feeling unhappy, dissatisfied, and disconnected from the real world."

If a day off to rest seems impossible, start smaller with regular digital sabbaticals. If you are heavily connected to your digital devices, start with an hour a day of being completely unplugged. If you are tempted to check e-mail or look at your phone, physically remove yourself from your devices. Go for a walk, or go out for lunch and leave them behind. Once you get comfortable, and perhaps begin to notice the benefits of disconnecting, try longer digital fasts like seven p.m. to seven a.m. Work your way to a full twenty-four hours a week of freedom, and longer when possible.

CHAPTER TWENTY-FIVE

Playing Guitar with My Amigos

I read "The Story of the Mexican Fisherman" long before I was ready to slow down, but it stayed with me. The seed was planted. I'd think of it from time to time when I was struggling to get ahead, or climbing another ladder. Even while I was living a very different story, this one was pinned to my bulletin board in my office, in my house, next to sales reports and goal sheets from my job, reminding me of what was most important. "The Story of the Mexican Fisherman" was originally told by Heinrich Böll and there are many different versions, but this is the simplest and my favorite:

> *An American businessman was at the pier of a small coastal Mexican village when a small boat with just one fisherman docked. Inside the small boat were several freshly caught fish. The businessman asked the fisherman how long it took to catch them as he admired the fish.*

The Mexican replied, "Only a few hours each day." The American then asked why didn't he stay out longer and catch more fish. The Mexican said he had enough to take care of his family. The American then asked, "But what do you do with the rest of your time?"

The Mexican fisherman said, "I sleep late, fish a little, play with my children, take siestas with my wife, Maria, stroll into the village each evening where I sip wine and play guitar with my amigos. I have a full and happy life."

The American scoffed. "I have a business degree and could help you. You should work harder, catch more fish, make more money, and then buy a bigger boat. With the proceeds from the bigger boat, you could buy several boats; eventually, you would have a fleet of fishing boats. Instead of selling your catch to a middleman you would sell directly to the processor, eventually opening your own cannery. You would control the product, processing, and distribution. You would need to leave this little village and move to Mexico City, then LA, and eventually New York City, where you will run your growing business."

The Mexican fisherman asked, "But how long will all this take?"

To which the American replied, "Fifteen to twenty years."

"But what then?" asked the Mexican.

The American laughed and said, "That's the best part. When the time is right you would announce an IPO and sell your company stock to the public and become very rich—you would make millions!"

"Millions—then what?"

The American said, "Then you would retire. Move to a small coastal fishing village where you would sleep late, fish a little, play with your kids, take siestas with your wife, stroll *to the village in the evenings where you could sip wine and play your guitar with your amigos."*

Every time I read this, I feel moved to live more simply so I can direct my love and energy to what matters most. I've learned so much from this story, including the following lessons:

1. **Stories are powerful.**
This little story inspired change in my life and work and still makes me think about what matters most. The original version was about an encounter between an enterprising tourist and a small fisherman on a European coast, in which the tourist suggests how the fisherman can improve his life. It's been told, retold, and adapted. You have so much to offer the world by sharing who you are, what you've experienced, and what it all means to you. Let's keep sharing meaningful stories.

2. **Change takes time.**
Even though I was working to make more and own more when I found this story, it kept working on me. When I'd look at my sales numbers, my eyes would run over these words. I wasn't ready at first, but I was curious and then I was committed. As I ventured into my soulful simplicity, this story gave me great inspiration to change. If there is a story working on your heart, give it room and take the time you need. It will be there when you are ready.

3. **Small is beautiful.**
In "The Story of the Mexican Fisherman," a small boat provided a beautiful life. You don't need an impressive title, big

car (or boat), or big business to live a beautiful life and be a beautiful person. In my experience, a smaller living space and fewer obligations have made life even sweeter.

4. **You already have it all.**
   If you have a nagging feeling that you could do better, make more, and deserve to upgrade, remember that the secret to having it all is recognizing that you already do.

5. **Advice is nice, but intuition is better.**
   The Harvard grad had plenty of advice, but the fisherman knew what was best. Read, research, listen to advice, and then do what you know will be best for your life. If you don't know, make time and space to listen, because you probably do know, but have been too busy/stressed/ worried to trust your voice. Your hands-on-heart practice will help.

6. **The time is now.**
   Do you want to enjoy your work and life now or work a job you hate and endure a stressful life so you might find joy in twenty years? It has to start now. That doesn't mean that everything has to change immediately, but start building joy into your life today. You deserve that.

7. **You can't put a price on a good life.**
   Not even a million dollars.

8. **Spend time with your amigos.**
   The wife, children, and amigos were all an integral part of the fisherman's life. Spend time with people who lift

you up, lift them right back, and quietly distance yourself from those who don't.

I don't have a bulletin board, an office, or a house anymore. I don't have the job with the sales reports and goals either. Instead, I have a happy marriage, thriving soul-centered business, and time to enjoy coffee, writing, or a hike with my amigos. Instead of a big job, big car, and big expense account, I have a big, beautiful life and I'm so grateful. Live small so you can live big.

CHAPTER TWENTY-SIX

The Art of No-ing

Saying no is an art. Think about what goes into saying no. It involves knowing and honoring what you want, appreciating the request or opportunity, and letting go of people pleasing, to name just a few elements. As with all art, you have to practice saying no before you get comfortable with it. Saying no is one of the most practical things we can do to create more time to engage in what matters most. Even though we may feel bad or worried about saying no, it's still important, because we need more time than we think. Not only do we need time to do the usual things, but we need time to notice things and to process thoughts and emotions. We need time to move through the world, present and undistracted. We need time to just be. We need time to remember who we are. We can better serve the world when we have time to respond thoughtfully instead of reacting mindlessly. We need time to take care of our bodies, and time to listen to our hearts. We deserve time to engage in the things that are on our heart lists, not only the things on our to-do lists. Things like taking a long walk or doodling in a notebook. We need time to call someone just to laugh and chat, time to dip our toes in the ocean or a lake, and time to disconnect from the Internet for a few days. It takes time to take care of our bodies, brains, hearts, and souls, and if we don't take that time, we can't take care of anyone else, at least not very well and not for very long. Continuing to serve everyone but ourselves will drain us and there will be consequences.

When all of your free time and space is dedicated to keeping up, catching up, regrouping, and making ends meet, it's not free time. If you want free time—real free time—or if you crave eight whole hours of sleep, a proper lunch break, or at least twenty-four hours away from your e-mail, you are going to have to say no. A lot. Saying no is no easy feat, especially for kind, generous souls, for people pleasers, and for people who are used to saying yes to everything. Here are a few of the usual suspects:

- Yes, I'll chair the silent auction.
- Yes, I'll meet you for coffee.
- Yes, I'll make a wonderful family dinner.
- Yes, you can pick my brain.
- Yes, I'll drive you to the airport.
- Yes, I'll take that call.
- Yes, I'll make that thing for that party.
- Yes, I'll respond to every notification on my phone.

And the list goes on and on and on.

We've all said yes when we wanted to say no. Whether we said it out of guilt, for fear of missing out, or to please others, it's important to note that saying yes when your heart says no is a disservice not only to you but to everyone you say yes to. If your heart says no, it will fight the yes all the way through. You won't be excited to contribute. You won't give your best, and you may end up resenting the commitment or the person who asked you to commit.

If you struggle to say no and protect your time, consider some of these techniques in the art of no-ing:

1. **Be grateful and graceful while saying no.** Jonathan Fields suggests practicing the loving no in *How to Live a Good Life: Soulful Stories, Surprising Science, and Practical Wisdom*. Fields says to ask yourself, "How can I be kind and respectful yet also stand strong in what I need? What would that sound like?" He suggests picturing yourself spending all the time you've now freed up doing the thing that really matters to you before responding with your no. Be grateful for the invitation, respectful of the time and courage it may have taken someone to ask, and graceful and loving when you decline.

2. **Be clear.** Saying things like "let me think about it" is often a delaying tactic. When you know it's a no, say no. If you want to say yes, but the timing is bad, suggest another time and be specific.

3. **Keep it short.** Author Anne Lamott says, "No is a complete sentence." Expand when you need to, but still keep it short. In just a few sentences, you can say no with gratitude. "No thank you. I appreciate you thinking of me, but I have another commitment" is better than a long explanation about how busy and sorry you are.

4. **Do your most important work first.** If the first thing you do in the morning is check e-mail, you may never have a chance to decide what's most important to you. Put your oxygen mask on first.

5. **Say "Hell Yeah!"** Derek Sivers's approach to feeling like you are doing too much is this: "Those of you who often over-commit or feel too scattered may appreciate a new philosophy I'm trying: If I'm not saying 'HELL YEAH!' about something, then say no. Meaning: When deciding whether to commit to something, if I feel anything less than, 'Wow! That would be amazing! Absolutely! Hell yeah!'—then my answer is no. When you say no to most things, you leave room in your life to really throw yourself completely into that rare thing that makes you say 'HELL YEAH!' We're all busy. We've all taken on too much. Saying yes to less is the way out."

6. **Try a yes fast.** If it's impossible for you to say no, or to know when to say no or when to say yes, try a yes fast. Make a commitment to say no to every request for thirty days. Practice the loving no over and over again. Share your challenge with others, not as a built-in excuse, but to inspire them to respect their time and what matters to them too.

7. **Dump the guilt.** Of course, you will help someone in their time of need, so dump the guilt around not baking cookies, attending an event, or picking someone up from

the airport at midnight. Believe in yourself and what you know is best for your life and say no to guilt.

8. **Know what matters.** You are faced with endless options and decisions, but very little of it really matters to you. Keep simplifying and creating more time for yourself and you'll become even more connected to what does. It is in the small, silent moments that you build your strength and resilience so you can contribute to the world in more meaningful ways. When you sit quietly and put your hands on your heart, you'll know what matters most.

Soulful Streamlining

> *Take a deep breath. Get present in the moment and ask yourself what is important this very second.*
>
> —GREG MCKEOWN, *Essentialism*

We make thousands of decisions every day. While some of those decisions are intuitive, others require more problem solving and mental bandwidth. All of the choosing often leads to decision fatigue. It starts first thing in the morning. Should I get up or hit the snooze button? Coffee or shower first? What should I wear? Do those shoes go with these pants? Cereal or eggs for breakfast? Do I even want breakfast? We are fortunate to have the freedom to choose, but according to Barry Schwartz, author of *The Paradox of Choice: Why More Is Less*, we aren't happier because of it. Schwartz says, "When people have no choice, life is almost unbearable. As the number of available choices increases, as it has in our consumer culture, the autonomy, control, and liberation this variety brings are powerful and positive. But as the number of choices keeps growing, negative aspects of having a multitude of options begin to appear. As the number of choices grows further, the negatives escalate until we become overloaded. At this point, choice no longer liberates, but debilitates."

If we were making fewer decisions, could we make better decisions? I've experimented with living and dressing with less and entertaining fewer options and the answer I've discovered is a resounding yes. When we create boundaries around things that are distracting us from what really matters, our level of engagement in the things we actually care about becomes boundless.

You can relieve decision fatigue and be better equipped for those days of endless decisions with soulful streamlining. Automate your decision making. Free up some of that precious mental energy for other decisions and engagement. Here's how:

1. **Start with food.** We make choices about food every day, and if you add restaurant choices, menu items, when you should eat, where to eat, and why you are hungry to the 47,000 other choices at the grocery store, you start to get an idea of how this decision fatigue thing works. Instead, shop the perimeter of the store, eat similar meals every day, and don't food shop without a list or a plan.

2. **Pretend the Internet is broken.** Bored? Play an Internet game. Lost? Google it. Lonely? Find friends on Facebook. The Internet has endless options and choices that trick us into believing that a workable solution is only a click away (and then another and another). The problem is we don't get to discover the solutions that come from being bored, lost, or lonely. Creativity and clarity are squashed with too many answers and choices. Too much choosing is a

problem. Tell your family that the Internet is broken on Sundays or whatever day works for you and take a digital break.

3. **Take back your inbox.** E-mail creates a plethora of decisions to be made. Respond? Delete? Hit send? Read all the way through? Say yes? Say no? All of the questions and ideas that arrive via e-mail occupy your brain and muddle up your early morning clarity. While there are systems out there to alleviate e-mail stress, the best way to take control is to open your inbox only one to three times a day.

4. **Ask for help.** Instead of tormenting yourself trying to make a decision, or worse, avoiding the decision altogether because you are too scared or overwhelmed to choose, ask someone for help (especially if you are tired or stressed). Sometimes letting someone else weigh in adds great clarity to your decision. Note: Feedback from one or two people will be enough. Don't form a committee or make asking for help another form of procrastination.

5. **Undo your to-do list.** The reason we don't know how to prioritize is because there is so much to do that we can't identify how we want to spend our time. Passions and interests are buried somewhere on page 3 of our to-do lists. These never-ending lists are winning. They never get done, only rewritten. All of that time consumed with listing the things to do and feeling bad about the things that were left undone contributes to the lack of time you have to do them. Instead, keep one master to-do list.

Before you go to sleep, pull one to three items that you'll do tomorrow. When you finish them, revisit the list or take a walk.

6. **Consider that unrounded kids are pretty awesome too.** Violin lessons for focus, team sports for persistence, tutoring sessions for perfection, and other activities to round out our kids go on and on. We are creating résumés for children for a life they probably don't want. Kids and parents are exhausted. Pick one activity instead of all the activities. Instead of making kids well rounded, let's make them loved and loving.

7. **Create a decision-free closet.** How many decisions a day are fashion based? When mornings are consumed with choosing outfits and weekends spent at the mall looking for deals and trends, we become slaves to fashion, even if we don't really care about fashion. Create a capsule wardrobe and choose from a very small selection seasonally. I recommend thirty-three items or less.

8. **Habit stack your morning routine.** If you know how you will spend the first few hours of each day, and you spend it engaged in healthy habits, you'll reduce decision fatigue before you even get out of bed in the morning. See chapter 19 for details on creating your morning routine.

9. **Eliminate what doesn't matter.** If you want to know what really matters to you, eliminate everything that doesn't. Simplifying things creates an environment that requires fewer choices, and leaves more energy and focus

for making the decisions that we need to make. When we give things up and let things go, we might miss out on some of it, but we won't care because we will be so happy that we are surrounded by and immersed in our favorite things and we are making decisions that offer greater benefit than choosing the perfect cereal for breakfast.

10. **Come back to your heart practice.** Create and honor the moments when you can connect with your heart. Keep coming back. Keep asking, "Does this matter?" If you want to do more than skim the surface of the most important parts of your life, create a life with fewer decisions and distractions. It will dramatically improve your health, work, and relationships.

CHAPTER TWENTY-SEVEN

Reclaim the Lost Art of Lingering

Even just hearing the word *linger* encourages me to slow down, notice my surroundings, and drink them in. I'm guessing the woman I mentioned in chapter 20 who set her microwave in the most time-efficient way didn't do much lingering. Do any of us? This thing we have about measuring who we are by what we get accomplished is really messing up our ability to let go and linger. For a long time, I couldn't linger without a glass of wine. I just couldn't let go without something to help me loosen up. If I tried, my mind would race, obsessing about what wasn't getting done, about what my husband would think of my lack of ambition, about falling down the corporate ladder as others climbed over and ahead of me. It never occurred to me that working less would help me work and live more thoughtfully and more effectively. When I banned my phone from my car, stopped checking e-mail every ten minutes, and saw improvement in my work, I thought maybe there was something to this idea of pulling back. If you (like me) like to give your all, please consider what it would feel like if you gave your all less 5 or 10 percent. Would anyone really notice? Is there a chance if you devoted that 5 or 10 percent to lingering that your quality of contribution might improve? If you don't have time to linger or think you are too busy to slow down, connect with loved ones, and take care of your heart, or whenever you are thinking about how you spend your time, author Laura Vanderkam suggests, "Instead of saying 'I don't have time' try saying 'it's not a priority,'" and see how that feels.

When I think about lingering, I'm reminded of a scene from Elizabeth Gilbert's *Eat, Pray, Love*. She is in Italy, one of the three countries she chose to live in over the course of a year. This is the "eat" country—where she rediscovers pleasure. She is sitting in a barber shop in Italy with friends. She says she feels a little guilty because all she has done for three weeks is "learn a few Italian words and eat." (Sounds delightful, right?) Her Italian friend tells her she feels guilty because she is American and Americans are always busy and burned out, not knowing pleasure because they have to be told they've earned it. His solution? The Italian practice of dolce far niente—"the sweetness of doing nothing." When was the last time you let time slip away and lingered over something? Perhaps it was a meal, or spending time with someone you don't see very often. Maybe you lingered over a book and went to bed much later than planned. Or perhaps you can't remember the last time. Have you lost the art of lingering?

YOU KNOW YOU HAVE LOST THE ART OF LINGERING WHEN YOU . . .

- walk through a museum like you walk to your gate in an airport
- wrap dinner early to catch your favorite TV show

- take your dog for a walk to the mailbox instead of the park
- eat at your desk, typing with one hand
- type with both hands, brushing crumbs off your keyboard
- skip yoga to do extra work
- jump out of bed and head right to the shower or the coffee machine
- won't make slow-cook oatmeal because it's too slow

I couldn't identify these pitfalls unless I had fallen into them myself before. Most of us grow up learning that getting it done is more important than enjoying, lingering, and letting one moment inform the next. A jam-packed schedule may include drive-through meals, a calendar with no white space, driving too fast, cell phones on in the car, anxiety, reactive behavior instead of a thoughtful response, impulse shopping, one-way conversations, and missed opportunities to engage and enjoy. No dolce far niente.

You owe it to yourself and your loved ones to start embracing life and stop living just to get it all done, because when it's all done . . . it's all done. Think about the moments you miss every day because you are on autopilot. Just reflect on yesterday. Walk through the day in your mind. What happened, moment by moment? Can you recall conversations, or other things that happened, or is it all a blur? Now shift to thinking about moments you can begin to enjoy by waking up a few minutes earlier, dropping an obligation that has no meaning to you, and turning off the TV. Think about how you feel when you are on vacation (unless you are an obsessive planner with an itinerary for every day). When you take a vacation, you leave everything behind and sometimes don't even pay attention to time. By the end of your stay, you are relaxed and happy. You might notice that you are more aware of what's going on around you and can stay focused for longer periods of time.

You can infuse some of that clarity and softness into your everyday life by reclaiming the lost art of lingering. Working more, longer, harder so you can afford your next vacation is not the answer. Incorporating vacation behavior into your life every day is the better choice. This will take practice, intention, and a commitment to reprioritize, but what happens when you are successful is that you enjoy life more, and as a side effect become more loving, creative, and productive. You can begin to work smarter instead of harder.

Practical Ways to Reclaim the Lost Art of Lingering

Linger first. When you wake up in the morning, breathe and stretch. Look out the window before you look at your computer or phone. Smile. Set the stage for the whole day with a slower morning.

Take a long lunch. Schedule a lunch date for yourself. Go alone or bring a friend. Resist the urge to check your phone—even better, leave your phone at home or turn it off. Enjoy a sparkling water or glass of champagne. Feel the bubbles on your tongue. If you are sitting in the sunshine, appreciate the warmth on your skin. Order and enjoy one menu item at a time. Savor each bite.

Create for thirty minutes. Try drawing even if you don't know how to draw or try an adult coloring book. Don't worry about technique or any sort of perfection, just make something with your hands and your heart. During your next thirty-minute creativity session, give painting or writing a shot. Give yourself the time and permission to linger over creativity. For more inspiration to create, read *The Artist's Way* by Julia Cameron. Working my way through her beautiful book and recommendations several times over the last twenty years is the reason I write and create today.

Plan a meal. Nourish your body and your soul with a slow-cooked meal. Choose a recipe that requires your attention. Turn on music that helps you melt into the moment (for me that's Diana Krall) and slowly chop vegetables, stir sauces, and set the table. Light candles and call friends or family for dinner. If it's just you, sit at the table and admire what you've created. Turn down the lights, ban cell phones and electronics from the room, and let everyone know that the dishes can wait. If you have successfully reclaimed the lost art of lingering, you will spend more time at the table enjoying your meal than you did creating it.

Take a coffee break. Anna Brones and Johanna Kindvall celebrate the Swedish coffee break in their book *Fika: The Art of the Swedish Coffee Break*. They describe it this way: "Functioning as both a verb and a noun, the concept of fika is simple. It is the moment that you take a break, often with a cup of coffee, but alternatively with tea, and find a baked good to pair with it. You can do it alone, you can do it with friends. You can do it at home, in a park or at work. But the essential thing is that you do it, that you make time to take a break: that's what fika is all about."

They say it's more than a coffee break—it's a moment to slow down and appreciate the good things in life. It's lingering.

Take a little walk. In Italy, in almost every town, village, and city, people come out for the evening stroll called *la passeggiata*. It means "little walk." They aren't out to burn calories or build muscle tone or even to reduce stress. They take a little walk to see and be seen and to be a part of their community. They linger over one another. The next time you finish dinner, instead of rushing to get the dishes done or to get the kids ready for bed, or finish your work, take a little walk and really see each other. Adopt *la passeggiata* no matter where you live.

My parents moved to Italy in 2012, and when they did, I looked forward to lingering there. Even though I had started to linger at home, I really wanted to do it in Italy as a thank-you to Elizabeth Gilbert, my dolce far niente inspiration. As we walked miles through Milan, Florence, Tuscany, and finally Rome I didn't search for sunglasses, or shop for trinkets to memorialize the trip. I lingered instead. I closed my eyes and really tasted the red wine and pizza at lunch. I listened to coffee beans as they were turned into the perfect espresso. I got lost in the smiles on people's faces as they threw coins in the Trevi fountain and made their great wishes. I loved lingering in these renowned Italian cities, but it was the little walks in Arezzo where I experienced the real meaning of dolce far niente.

The greatest treasures from my trip to Italy weren't things, but fully engaged experiences like sitting around beautifully set dinner tables, helping my mom hang laundry on her balcony with a view of the rolling Tuscan hills, and walking through narrow cobblestone streets. The treasures were laughter, train rides, art, and connection. Once you connect with and identify your real treasures, and take the time to linger longer, you'll see that the rest is just stuff, and you can finally let it go.

CHAPTER TWENTY-EIGHT

Adopt the Pace of Nature

When I reflect on the times when I was living outside of myself, and not remembering who I was, I understand why I lived there for so long. I wasn't present, or at least not very often. I kept myself busy, and distracted, and focused on everything but the moment I was in. Everything I did was a stepping-stone for the next thing. I rarely did one thing for the sake of the one thing, but for a bigger goal. I fought for my place in the future and worried about the uncertainty of what was to come. This made it impossible for me to stay where I was, or be connected to who I was. Some may struggle with the past. Holding on to guilt and regret or wondering what would have been prevents us from engaging in what's right in front of us.

Other things keep us unengaged too. Things like distraction, busyness, feeling overwhelmed, exhausted, and sick. How can we be here, feeling our feet rooted to the earth, and our hearts connected in conversation, when we are worried about what's next on our to-do lists, what we've left undone, and where we are going to find the energy to catch up and the means to make ends meet. Combine those internal distractions with the phone notifications, Facebook updates, and other external distractions and it becomes increasingly clear why being present must be an intentional practice and not something we expect to happen naturally. I'm guilty of looking down at my phone mid-conversation, or getting lost in my own thoughts, but my soulful simplicity has allowed me to bounce back faster, to recognize the disconnection, and to create an environment with less distraction and more connection. A soulful simplicity helps you create time and space, but also more attention for the moment you are in, or at least the ability to recognize how meaningful it is to stay in the moment. When you are present, you are connected: connected to the people around you, to your work, or to whatever it is you are experiencing.

Connection is one benefit of presence. Another is under-reacting. Overreacting never comes from a calm, peaceful, present place. Anytime I've overreacted, I wasn't present. I was distracted, tired, or removed in another way. I wasn't really there. For a while I thought I was creating time to do more, but what I was really doing was creating the presence of mind to show up. To show all the way up.

Adopt the Pace of Nature

Presence requires patience. Ralph Waldo Emerson said, "Adopt the pace of nature: her secret is patience." By taking walks, hiking, and watching the sunrise, I see that the most beautiful, magical things in life go at their own pace. No matter how many times I tried to will other people to move faster and get out of my way so I could get on with my busy day, it never worked. Even my most powerful attempts failed over and over again. Instead, I just got frustrated. I was annoyed with the slow drivers, the people who wanted to write a check at the grocery store, first-time travelers going through security lines, and coworkers who weren't prepared at meetings. Why couldn't everyone move at my pace?

My hurry melted into patience one December afternoon at the post office. There was a big line, only one person working, and a woman in front of me who decided to take her time picking out the perfect stamp. I was annoyed. Couldn't she pick a stamp already? When she was finally finished, she turned around and recognized the woman standing behind me. They hadn't seen each other in a while and discovered in a moving conversation I couldn't help but overhear that they both had lost their husbands to cancer over the last month. The woman was picking stamps for thank-you notes she was sending to people who attended her husband's funeral. Tears of compassion, sadness, and embarrassment for my hurry pooled in my eyes. Before they exchanged one last hug, one of the women said to the other, "Now we can be alone together." With that, I forgot my rush. I held that moment and those women in my heart, and I'll never forget that exchange.

Aside from slowing the pace of my own life and boycotting busyness, what helps me most when it comes to being patient is thinking of people as people. When someone is taking too long to pick out stamps, she isn't someone out to get me or ruin my day. She's a brokenhearted woman who lost her husband, picking out the perfect stamps to honor him.

CHAPTER TWENTY-NINE

Put Your Hands on Your Heart

Here we are again. If you are just beginning your hands-on-heart practice, visit the hands-on-heart chapters in sections one and two for more detailed instructions on getting started. If you've been practicing as you've been reading, you may notice that it's getting easier to sit still, or that you are looking forward to your next heart session. Or perhaps your practice hasn't been as smooth. If it's been a struggle to know what questions to ask your heart or to sit still and wait for answers, you are not alone. Even though I've been practicing for years, there are times when three minutes feels like an eternity and other times when I never want the conversation to stop. I combine my hands-on-heart practice with other meditation or writing, and if the practice doesn't feel right, I spend more time writing or sitting quietly. It's not important that your practice is easy, or that answers come flooding out every time. Just keep showing up. Keep connecting with your heart.

Jess Lively, a podcaster and online teacher specializing in

intuition, has a practice of writing to her intuition. She questions her intuition when she is faced with uncertainty and documents her conversations for clarity on different situations in her life and work. Following is the letter she wrote when she was considering selling her home and most of her belongings to travel and work from different locations around the world.

· · ·

Dear Intuition,

What should I know about this situation? *You are loved.*

I'm scared. *I know you are.*

Why? *Because you think you can do this perfectly and you can't.*

What do you mean? *You want all the ducks in a row.*

How are they not in a row? *You don't know where you are going to live next.*

Is this your will for me? *My will is for you to love.*

For as cryptic as this seems, at the same time, everything has unfolded in incredible fluidity.

There have been no snags or hold ups. *That is because this is what you want.*

Is it? *Yes.*

Why? *Because you want a new life you never imagined before.*

I do? *Yes.*

Why? *Time will tell.*

Do you love me? *Yes. Unconditionally.*

Will I be okay? *Yes.*

Will I be safe? *You are never as safe as you think you will be.*

What would you have me do? *Go in faith.*

What about Ellie (my dog)? *Love her with all your heart.*

Thank you. Namaste.

· · ·

Jess didn't get crystal-clear answers and direction from her intuition, but she did get the reassurance she needed to move forward. She did sell her house and most of her belongings and has lived in London, Lisbon, and Cape Town, South Africa, over the last year, among other destinations. She is living *a new life she never imagined before.*

Suggested Questions for Making Time

Why am I so busy? It's easy to blame busyness on the demands of the day, but take a closer look. Why is it important for you to be and appear busy?

Is this important to me? When considering an invitation, ask the question, Is this important to me? so you can determine if you are saying yes for the right reasons.

What happens if this never gets done? Consider the items on your to-do list. What would happen if instead of procrastinating and moving your items to tomorrow's list, you crossed them off altogether? If you can't let it go, can someone help you do it?

How do I want to spend my precious time? Brainstorm ideas about how you really want to spend your minutes and moments.

MAKING TIME: ACTION STEPS

Work through this list in any order, trying one thing at a time.

Create a five-minute morning routine. Trade your snooze button for five minutes to engage in an activity you love. Five minutes won't feel like enough, but it's enough to start. If you want to practice longer than five minutes, resist.

Grow your morning routine with habit stacking. Add a new five-minute activity to your morning routine. In a week, stack another five-minute activity. Notice other habit-stacking routines in your day and see how each habit encourages the next.

Apply joyful discipline. If you struggle with your new habits or with sticking to a new routine, choose one of the recommendations from chapter 20 and add more joy to your structure and discipline.

Choose what goes on your plate. When you have a full plate, you have three choices:

1. Worry about everything on your plate and complain about how crazy busy you are.

2. Remove something from your plate to make room for something that matters more.

3. Recognize that your plate is full and say no to everything else so you can enjoy and engage in what is right in front of you.

Remember you have a choice.

Stop playing games with your time. Instead of saving seconds with a productivity hack, get your life back by slowing down and becoming more intentional about how you spend your time.

Boycott busy. Take the twenty-one-day busy boycott challenge detailed in chapter 21. Or visit bemorewithless .com/the-busy-boycott for a guided three-week challenge via e-mail.

Choose work that becomes you. Okay, so maybe this isn't a "small action," but take time to look at your work. Your life and work are deeply connected. Either they support each other or they don't. Are you thriving in your work, or have you become someone else to make it work? If necessary, consider a change.

Become a gentle warrior. Fight for your health, your love, and your life, but fight gently. Draw a line in the sand with your heart.

Put your phone down. Make eye contact and show people you see them and hear them. Your phone can wait. If you can't resist checking it when it's nearby, switch it off and keep it in another room.

Rest. Don't wait until your body forces you to rest by getting sick. Instead, rest regularly. Sleep well, take breaks.

Make a Sabbath box. Remove the things that keep you busy and distracted to encourage rest. Include your phone, tablets, and other digital devices. Mentally place things in the box that won't fit, like your washing machine, car, and other things that invite you into chores and busyness. Also include things left undone and worries by writing them on a piece of paper and placing it in the box. Close the box for a while and rest.

Say no. Protect your time and priorities by saying no. Ask your heart, "yes or no?" Trust the response. Remember, she knows things.

Practice soulful streamlining. Look for areas of your day that you can streamline to reduce decision fatigue. Start with food, your closet, and your morning routine.

Linger. Start spending more time at the dinner table than you spent making dinner. Savor every bite. Turn off the TV and stare at the stars.

Adopt the pace of nature. Be present. Be a part of your most precious moments simply by showing up for them.

MAKING LOVE:
WHAT REALLY MATTERS

Simplicity Is the Way Back to Love

It's always been about love. I didn't know it at first because I was so focused on the actions and mechanics of the changes I was making. I was looking at the how-to instead of the big picture. There was so much fear in the beginning that I could focus only on what was right in front of me. The future was scary. I was afraid of my declining health, afraid of money, afraid I'd be stuck at a job I didn't enjoy, afraid that I'd always be overwhelmed, distracted, and exhausted. It was hard to see love in all of that but with each little step, the fear dissipated. When I started to feel better and remember who I was, there was hope. With more space and less clutter came a lightness that served as an antidote to the fear. As I began to discover more time by cutting things out that weren't so important after all, and making a career change, I found freedom. Hope, light, and freedom were all wonderful side effects of simplicity, but the very best outcome is that I found my way back to love.

Love is so deeply intertwined in all of the changes you'll be making, in the person you are becoming, and in the life you are creating. Simplicity will transform your closet, your kitchen cabinets, and all of the spaces in your life, but all the while it will work on your heart too. Once all of the things that are weighing you down and holding you back are gone, all that's left is love.

A soulful simplicity will help you find your way back to love too.

CHAPTER THIRTY

Memory Boxes

I used to be the memory box girl. Every year starting in the fourth grade, I wrote in a locked diary and saved bits and pieces of my life in boxes. My parents were busy collecting my memories too. While I was storing notes from friends at school, my mom was diligently saving each report card and glowing teacher recommendation. They glowed less as the years went on, but she still kept them.

For decades, I carefully stored and carted around my memory boxes from home to home and state to state, even though most of the artifacts of my life offered no connection to anything real to me. These pieces of history that represented the high highs and low lows of my life failed to trigger the memories I had hoped to preserve. A few things did, but most of the objects I had kept were just scraps of paper and plastic that had long ago lost their meaning. All that time, I saved my past to fill my future, but really I was only compromising my present and my presence.

Until I started to get rid of my personal possessions, they were all important. By the time my simplicity journey began, I had moved at least ten times as an adult. Each move was a perfect opportunity to let go, but instead, I boxed and bubble-wrapped each thing to take with me. Each new home invited more shopping, more stuff, and eventually, more bubble wrap. There was one major problem with this strategy, though—because everything was important, nothing was.

Layer after layer of decluttering and letting go revealed what mattered to me. One example was my textbooks from Savannah College of Art and Design. I went to art school before computer graphics or e-mail existed. My love of art will always remain, but those books aren't relevant anymore. So why was I keeping outdated art books but not spending time drawing or taking photography classes?

With each "thing" that I gave up, my soul asked for more—not more stuff, but more of the feelings and actions that the stuff promised. Was it possible to get there without the stuff acting as a conduit? My soul wanted to make art and have time to be creative. I had to honor that, and the only way was to let go and make more space and time to nourish my soul. In order to fully embrace the joy in my life now and be present for the best bits and pieces of today, I had to stop holding on to my past. In some ways, I was attached to things of my past because I thought it was a way to hold on to relationships. When I saved things from a relationship, it was either because something in the relationship was unresolved that I hoped to fix in the future or because the relationship had been so good that I didn't think I'd be lucky enough to ever have that goodness again. I thought I could save the relationships by stuffing them in a box. How many relationships are you storing in your attic, garage, or under your bed? Love doesn't flourish in those hidden spaces.

Krissy Barker, a development leader for big nonprofits, has

saved every birthday card, wedding invitation, Christmas card, and birth announcement she has ever received. When her dad died unexpectedly from complications of heart surgery when she was twenty-six and her mom died eight years later after a six-month battle with pancreatic cancer, Krissy's box of cards became filled with more cards from the funerals and other things her parents left behind. When she began to declutter, she started with her boxes of saved cards. "The funny thing is that they were just sitting in a box in my closet. I never looked at them or read them," she says. She decided to read through all of the cards one last time and then let them go, with the exception of two birthday cards—one from her mom and one from her dad. She forgot they were there, so it was a moving surprise to find them as they both included touching, handwritten messages. She now keeps both cards in her nightstand drawer. By getting rid of the hidden boxes, she made room for the love that her parents shared with her in those notes and was able to deal with some of the grief that she hadn't known how to process when she was younger. She treasures the words and enjoys knowing that they are close to her heart.

When I got to my own final stages of decluttering, like Krissy, I sifted through each faded note, good and bad grades, letters from the tooth fairy, and other stuff left over from my childhood. Because I continued to save long into adulthood too, I had to go through a lot of things. I tossed photos from late nights with friends in my early twenties and found myself feeling grateful that we didn't have Facebook then or any digital memory of things that belong in the past. I tossed matchbooks, champagne corks, beach sand, and other odds and ends. I saved a few things that made me smile, and let go of most of the things that reminded me of hurt and sadness. It was like going through each joyful and painful time again, item by item.

The memory works in mysterious ways. I could look at a note from someone who signed one of the five yearbooks I had been holding on to with no recollection of who they were, but walking through flower gardens in the foothills recently brought me right back to reading my favorite scratch-and-sniff book with my mom before I was even in school. When you are fully engaged in your present moments, in your relationships, and in your life, you'll remember things that meant something to you, and you will continue to accumulate beautiful memories. You will never run out. The memories will surface without a shrine of stuff built in their honor. You can't keep your relationships and memories in storage. Your past lives within you no matter what items you part with, and those items are mere representations of your past.

Dancers are a good example of how memories stay with us. When they learn new choreography, they don't just memorize steps and patterns. They absorb the work so that they don't have to think about it anymore and can just dance. They refer to it as "muscle memory," and the movements are mapped in the brain. If dance movement is mapped in the brain over a period of weeks or months, surely decades of our past memories are mapped not only in our brains but in our hearts and souls—every relationship and experience of our lives. No one can erase those memories, and no object can replace them. Your love stories, heartbreaks, tearful and joyous moments course through your veins, and when you need them most, they are available. It's when you silence your thoughts and memories with clutter that you can't recall what once meant something to you.

Sentimental items can be the most challenging to release, but remember that less isn't none. You don't have to give up all of it but it's good to consider how you might enjoy and appreciate what you do keep. I understand how emotional this process is. I'm sentimental and easily moved to tears. I get teary driving past a wedding, hearing stories about my grandparents when they were young, or cooking one of my favorite dishes from childhood. I know all too well that sorting through your sentimental items will spark powerful emotions, including sadness and fear, but those emotions cannot compete with the strength of your love. You are so much more than what you own or don't own. If you want a joyful life that is full of love and happiness, align your actions with your heart. Our hearts know that our real treasures are not in the attic or contained in any physical thing. Our hearts know that real treasures are smiles, tears, moments, and people.

When I first sifted through my memory boxes of ticket stubs and love letters, my mind wasn't present anymore. I wanted to put it all back in the box and come back to it another day . . . or year. I didn't think I was ready to let go. In an effort to hold on tight, I thought, "It's not hurting anything or anyone to keep this stuff." Then I remembered that I want my quality of life to be more in line with "How is this helping?" instead of "How is this not hurting?" I wanted to create an environment that allowed me to be fully present. Instead of lingering in the past, I wanted to be right in the middle of my big, beautiful life to laugh with my daughter, plan date nights with my husband, explore new cities, dip my toes in the ocean, work with awesome people, and send new love letters. Once I identified why I wanted to let it all go, the paper and plastic stuff that made up my memories didn't have a hold on me or on my heart anymore. Now, instead of capturing moments and boxing them up, I embrace and absorb them.

No One Wants Your Stuff

I receive e-mail after e-mail from people who struggle to let go. Parents e-mail me about saving things for their children and children e-mail me asking how they can tell their parents they don't want their stuff. In most cases, the simple yet sometimes hard truth is that your children don't want your stuff. They just want you. Make it easy for them by paring down now so that they aren't faced with the difficulty of dealing with your sentimental items later. Lynne Hite is an educator and consultant for the spa industry in Bend, Oregon, and the mother of two teenage boys. When her husband came home after visiting his deceased mother's house, he brought a truckload of her stuff with him. It sat in their garage for months, and finally, Lynne suggested he honor his mother's memory by choosing a few items to display on a bookshelf in the living room. He was then able to let go of her stuff, along with some of his grief, and begin to remember the moments he loved most with his mom.

I don't want my legacy to be storage containers of stuff. In one hundred years, no one will care about a letter of recommendation I received from an art professor that meant so much to me in 1992. No one will care how excited I was to get a ticket to a sold-out concert at the last minute or that my favorite drummer autographed it. The stuff won't matter, but the stories will. I have my stories, and I'll tell them to people who care. And they will tell them to other people who care. When I go, I want to be remembered for how I loved while I was here.

CHAPTER THIRTY-ONE

You Don't Have a Record Player

My parents moved to Italy when they retired, and they took most of their stuff with them. I thought it would be a good time to let go of some things, but for them, it was a time to hold on. One time when they were back in the United States visiting, we went out for lunch. While we were eating my mom mentioned that she was going to pick up my uncle's albums and FedEx them to Italy from Utah. My uncle had Down syndrome and had died a few years before, and one of his favorite things to do was listen to music. He collected record albums and organized them with a very detailed system that no one understood but him. He couldn't read, and the albums weren't sorted by genre or alphabetically, but if you asked him to find a particular album, he could put his hands on it without a second thought. A friend stored the albums for my mom when she moved.

I asked my mother why she would spend all of that money to ship heavy albums to Italy when it would be a big financial investment, she didn't have a record player, and she'd probably have to ship them back to the United States someday. I knew those albums would just sit in a box, and it was frustrating to me that she didn't think about the logistics. She changed the subject, but I wasn't ready to let it go. I tried to convince her that they weren't important or that bringing one album would be more meaningful than bringing all of them. Later that evening, when I got home, I thought about my compelling argument and quickly realized that it wasn't up to me to tell her what's important to her. I should have been gentler and more understanding, especially when I remembered that the albums weren't albums to her. They were memories of her brother. My mom wasn't thinking logically because she wanted to hold on to her brother, and she probably thought my argument to let the albums go meant that I didn't care about her or my uncle. Since she believed that holding on to the stuff allowed her to hold on to the person, my eagerness to let go came across as not caring about him. She may have thought I'd feel the same way about her stuff, which meant I didn't care about her either, or that I wouldn't miss or remember her one day.

We can have conversations and make recommendations, but we can't tell other people what they should keep or let go of, and only you can decide what matters most to you among your objects. A few months later on another visit, I overheard a friend of my mom's thanking her for the albums. She gave them away after all. I can only imagine how painful that was for her, but I could see the joy in her eyes when she realized that she had made someone else happy with the gift.

The incident made me realize that I should tell her more often about the times I think about her and about my dad, and how my memories and love for them are not tied to stuff. Like when I walked through the flower gardens remembering how she used to read to me when I was little, or how baking her Christmas cookie recipes reminds me of how she would let me help her bake, and sneaking little bites of batter in between the baking. I think of my dad whenever I hear music from one of the many concerts we attended from Squeeze to the Grateful Dead, and every time I see a rainbow. And in between those magical memories and moments, they are both always a part of me.

My lack of interest in my uncle's albums might have come across as not caring about people, but that's mostly all I care about now. Letting go of stuff has given me the space to care even more about people. By creating a soulful simplicity, I don't need sentimental items to be a sentimental person. I don't need things to remind me of my parents or the other people who have shaped my life—the people who loved me when I wasn't always deserving. I hear their voices, see their souls, and feel them in my heart.

CHAPTER THIRTY-TWO

Your Heart's Mission Statement

Author Jonathan Fields shared this humbling story about leading a class of yoga teachers at a yoga teacher training retreat: *"2002. Mexican Riviera. I'm sweating, almost violently. . . . Barefoot in the middle of a tiled, thatched-roof palapa feet from the rolling surf. I'm there with yoga wunderkind, Baron Baptiste, famed kirtan singer, Krishna Das, aka KD, and 100 sweaty humans training to become yoga teachers. We practice. We teach. We move. We twist. We grind. We stretch. We shake. Until we can no longer move. My head is pounding. Fruit is abundant. But all I want is caffeine. And a fan. On the last day, something's different. Baptiste begins to call postures. Minutes in, his number two takes over the call. Up dog. Down dog. Fingers wide. Palms kiss the mat. He tags number three, who takes us through the next Sun Salutation. I see the pattern and know what's coming. Three others on his team take the teaching baton as we flow, a hundred nubile bodies, pose-by-pose through the soupy morning. Baron steps in to lead us again. But I've done the*

*math. Ninety minutes remain. Who will lead? I stand in Namaskar.
Mountain Pose, erect at the mat's edge. Hands in prayer as the Universe sweats through me. I look at Baron. I want to go first. His eyes
catch mine. He smiles. Nods. I step off my mat and begin to stalk the
room. Inhale, I incant. The next few minutes are surreal. I've never
led a group this size through anything quite like this. I'm overwhelmed. I'm new at this. But I own my own studio back home.
Damned if I'm not already good. Better than most. Or so I think. I
finish the sequence and step back to my mat. Baptiste looks. 'Less
show,' he says, 'more soul.' I'm pissed. It would take years for me to
own the truth of his words. Show is soul's cover-up. It's been a lesson
hard learned. So much bravado. So much posturing. Positioning. All
to distract from the simple fact that you really don't quite know who
you are. Or what you're doing. And the last thing you want is for
others to know, too."*

Show is soul's cover-up. Think about all the times you've
hidden your soul with an act, a little show. Now that we are
getting rid of the clutter, debt, and busyness, next up to go is the
show. It's time to drop the act. No more show. No more shiny and
admired, only real and loved. All soul. The more you work to remember yourself, the easier this is, but it's still hard. It will help to
get very clear about who you are and what you want by creating a
mission statement for and from your heart.

Get Clear on Your Mission

Create a mission statement as a personal guide for working and
living your soulful truth. Don't use fancy words or Google "how
to write a mission statement." Instead, put your hands on your
heart, close your eyes, and listen. Then write about what's important to you. Include who you are, and what you do to support

that. You can share your heart's mission statement, but you are writing this for you. Once you articulate who you are and what matters to you, you'll have a better idea of how to align your actions with your heart.

MY HEART'S MISSION STATEMENT

I work toward full clarity on what is most important by getting rid of everything that isn't, and by saying no to things that don't matter. To matter, they must support health and/or love in my life. I create boundaries so that I am free to expand in the best directions and don't feel pressured to go in all directions.

I reject perfection, comparison, and competition. I don't resent the past, or let the future dictate the present. I am firmly rooted in the present, and to support that I take time to listen to my heart and feed my soul. The quiet messages from my heart and soul guide my decision making in life and work. I trust myself to know that what feels right and good usually is right and good.

I lift myself up with good food, meditation, movement, and creativity so I can lift the people around me, including my close friends and family and anyone else who needs something as simple as a smile, or as complex as massive change in their life, or work. In my work, I inspire people to simplify their work and lives so they can discover and enjoy what matters most to them, so they can find their way back to love.

Think of your mission statement as a soulful framework that guides you instead of a strict list of rules. My mission statement describes how I want to live, but like all humans, I forget. When I notice things are getting messy, I go back to basics and remind myself to start again. When I forget my soul and get caught up in the show, or begin to lose myself, I come back to my heart's mission statement. Then I remember.

Use Your Mission Statement to Serve . . .

YOU

Before you take care of anyone else, you have to serve yourself first. You have to put yourself before the people you serve at work and the people in your day-to-day life including family, friends, and community. Because to serve, you need something to offer, and if you are depleted, overwhelmed, and underinspired, your offering may be diluted or misleading. If you want to give your best, become your best.

FAMILY

These are the people we love and support, but also the people we often try to fix. Serving your family isn't always about fixing things or solving problems, it's about being there. The very best way to serve your family is to show up and be present. Be there. Eliminate the distractions that prevent you from seeing, hearing, and appreciating the people you love.

COMMUNITY

To serve your neighborhood, country, or the world, start by loving them. Then be honest enough to demonstrate your imperfections and weaknesses. Be open to giving and receiving love with people you don't know very well, might not understand, or don't agree with politically, spiritually, or otherwise. Learn from them and trust that when you serve them, they serve you right back.

WORK

When you put people first, you naturally build purpose into your work (even if you don't love your job). And when you get the combination of loving your work and serving people in alignment with what you care about . . . watch out, world.

CHAPTER THIRTY-THREE

The Victory Lap

I saved most of my sentimental items for last. I didn't get rid of all of them, but most. I kept a few pictures from my childhood, but let go of the red, sparkly dance outfit I wore when I was two. I said good-bye to my report cards, school projects, and yearbooks but turned my favorite photo of my grandparents into a bookmark so I can honor my memories of them when I read. Mark and I have a book of images from our wedding day, but the invitations, menu, and dried flowers are gone. We rarely look at our photo album, but we think of the day we were married when we walk by or attend a service in the church where we were married. I burn my journals each year while saving some stories and ideas digitally. Letting go gives me room to adore and appreciate what's right in front of me. If you are ready to consider letting go of sentimental items, try these three steps.

1. **Strengthen your ability to let go.**

   Don't start with the sentimental items. It took years before I was ready. First I had to build strength with letting go of the easier stuff like clothing, kitchen duplicates, sports- or hobby-related items that I didn't use anymore, and furniture. After years of building those muscles, I turned to items I felt more attached to like books and sentimental items. I had more strength to let go because of the benefits I had already experienced.

2. **Tell the story of your stuff.**

   Take pictures of your sentimental items or write about the reason you saved them. If you saved your daughter's first bathing suit, write the story about when she first dipped her toes in the salt water. Write about the time your grandmother taught you how to cook one of her favorite recipes from the cookbook you held on to. Tell your friends about why you saved a letter of recommendation from your favorite teacher. If you don't enjoy writing, make an audio or video recording of your stories. As you share the stories, you'll notice that the item isn't what your heart is holding on to. Your heart doesn't want to hold on to stuff. All she wants is love.

3. **Take a victory lap.**

   Blogger and online business strategist Sarah Von Bargen has a beautiful way of letting go of meaningful items. She says, "Like everyone else in the world, there are many, many things in my home that I'm struggling to part with because they're steeped in sentimental value.

My grandmother's vintage dresses, my mom's fondue pot, the scarf I bought while teaching English in Brazil—all these things are filled with meaning. My grandma's dresses are too cinched and fitted for my current style sensibilities, the fondue pot is too thin to be of much use, and that scarf doesn't match anything. After much thought, I created a process I call the 'victory lap.' I give each item one last intentional, loving use. I wear my grandmother's dress to Thanksgiving dinner and my aunts ooh and ahh over it. I ask my mom for her favorite cheese fondue recipe and then I invite friends over for a party in honor of melted cheese. I take my scarf on a tour of the art museum and out into the crisp fall air. Then I mentally thank that item for the role it played in my life, remind myself that an object is not a relationship and tuck it lovingly into the ever-present Goodwill donation bag in my front closet. It's a bit woo-woo, but I find it's a sweet way to honor the people who gave me these things while also honoring my own desire for a simpler, more pared-down life."

However you choose to let go, remember that less is not nothing. Display your sentimental items if they make you smile. Keep a few things for your children. Re-purpose charms into new jewelry, old watch parts into art, or faded love letters into a beautiful collage. Let go of sentimental items when you are ready, and make room to enjoy today and space for new memories and more love in a way that lifts your heart.

CHAPTER THIRTY-FOUR

You Are Written All over My Heart

In section one, I told you about my dog Guinness, how we found him, and how we fell in love. One afternoon, we noticed that Guinness was limping. He was a crazy, active dog, prone to getting into trouble, so we weren't that worried. After all, wasn't he the dog who got a bit too curious one day and ended up with porcupine quills in his nose and face?

Over the years, he had to have two surgeries, one on each back leg, but this is common for larger dogs, especially squirrel chasers like Guinness. Still, his limp continued to get worse, and we noticed that he put less and less weight on his right front leg. Aside from the limping, though, he never let us know he was hurting. Bailey and I took him to the vet, expecting a pulled muscle, a prescription for an anti-inflammatory, and doctor's orders for rest.

But it was worse than that—worse, in fact, than we could have imagined. Guinness was diagnosed with osteosarcoma, an aggressive form of bone cancer in dogs. The prognosis was grim. Ninety-five percent of dogs don't live past the six-month mark, but more immediate was the painful tumor in his leg. It had eaten away most of the bone, so it was only a matter of time before his leg would break. In the meantime, it meant terrible pain for our boy . . . and for all of us. He was just eight years old. We weren't ready. This was Guinness, my friend, my baby, my healer. We weren't ready. I wasn't ready.

Our options came down to saying good-bye or amputating his leg. After days of crying and trying to figure out what would be best for him, we decided to move forward with the amputation. Guinness had healed our family, and now it was our turn to heal him, or at least to give him all of the love and adventure he deserved. Mark had a T-shirt that said "May I become the person that my dog thinks I am." It always reminded me how this dog loved us no matter what. Guinness made us better people and taught us to be more loving with one another.

Even though the surgery wouldn't extend his life, it would give him three to six months of pain-free hiking on his favorite trails, lots of cuddling, treats, and whatever else we could do to thank him for lifting us up for so many years. If this had happened before we paid off our debt and downsized, we wouldn't have had the resources to move forward with the surgery without going deeper into debt or hiring someone to stay home with Guinness while I was at work.

One month after the amputation, he was back on his favorite trail. In that moment, we knew we had made the right decision. We went back to the vet at the three- and six-month marks for chest X-rays, bracing ourselves for the news that the cancer had spread to his lungs, but it never did. We like to think we loved and spoiled him so much that we scared the cancer off. Unfortunately, as the vet warned us, carrying eighty pounds on three legs can present other problems. All of his legs were affected, but his remaining front leg took the bulk of the pressure, and it started to break down. Almost a year after the surgery, instead of hiking, he could barely make the walk to the end of our street. He was declining faster than we could rehab his deteriorating leg. He was in pain and having more bad days than good, so almost a year after his surgery, we knew it was time to say good-bye.

The saying "Grief is the price we pay for love" is true. Loving and losing our dog showed me that my capacity for joy, love, grief, and pain is so much greater than I had thought. I'm also now acutely aware of what matters most in my life. By clearing the stuff, the distractions, and the things that didn't matter to me, I could love my family (including pets) and the other people in my life without condition. I'm able to give my attention to who and what matters most.

When we were making the final arrangements for Guinness, the vet clinic asked if we wanted a commemorative paw print, and through my tears, I smiled. I declined to add another object to our life of simplicity. I thought about the paw prints that are all over my life—on my furniture, my shoes, the patio, and everywhere else. No matter how much I clean, I'll find those paw prints for months to come. And when they fade or wash away, they will remain written all over my heart.

CHAPTER THIRTY-FIVE

Becoming a Saint

A soulful simplicity isn't tied to a certain religion or spiritual belief, but it can be if that interests you. I was born and raised Episcopalian, but as an adult, I've been a bit of a spiritual wanderer. I am curious about my relationship with God, but have trouble connecting with everything in the Bible, or subscribing to a set of ideas only because a group of people believes in it. I've been to lots of different churches and places of worship, studied and connected with people from different faiths, and done quite a bit of searching on my own. I've also spent many Sunday mornings hiking, skiing, and spending time with my family. Many of these outings have become their own spiritual adventures. I don't know the answers, but I do remember discovering that I could have a direct relationship with God without the middlemen. I liked that I could just show up and say hello like I did when I was five and knelt down beside my bed to say my prayers.

In all of my wandering, if I have to choose a house of worship, I always feel most at home in an Episcopal church. I fought that for a while, complaining about the ritualistic nature of the service, frustrated that I knew more about how to act in church than how to connect with God (more show than soul), but when the ritual was gone I missed it. It turns out that was part of the connection for me. The church I visit most frequently now is right around the corner from our apartment. Mark and I were married there and it's where Bailey attended church school.

For a while, Mark and I were attending a Sunday service at eight a.m. in the small chapel where we were married next to the grand cathedral. We didn't want the fuss of the mainstream service. We wanted the message. We also enjoyed sitting in the small, holy room where we once said "I do." One Sunday, Reverend Tyler Doherty was delivering the sermon. His words spoke to my soul. Each Sunday as I walked into the chapel, I said a little prayer that Tyler might be standing there to teach us. Tyler's sermon was about the raising of Lazarus. Now, I'll be honest, I don't know most of the Bible stories very well, and this wasn't a familiar one. Instead of paying attention to each tiny detail of the story, I was looking for the message that would resonate with me. What would he say that I could bring into my life, that I could bring into the world? After a few minutes, I could tell it was coming.

These are his words that my soul grabbed on to:

I think we sometimes have a rather puritanically distorted view of what it means to be a saint. On our wall at home, we have what the Eastern Orthodox call an iconostasis—a collection of icons that depict the life of Christ interspersed with various saints. Some of the saints on our wall include St. Seraphim of Sarov, Theophane the Recluse, St. Silouan the Athonite and other rather rigorously ascetic types. All lived lives of deep prayer, mostly in isolation, and attained great heights of personal holiness.

But as Laura Reilly was putting the finishing touches on the parish directory this past week, I got to thinking that perhaps that collection of faces from our very own parish, those icons, might serve as a different kind of iconostasis, one that celebrates the work of the Spirit in and through the blessedly ordinary and mixed-up lives of each one of us. For, in the final analysis, saints aren't the kind of people who live out a "ten-point plan to holiness" and hold to a rigid set of rules. There is no one pattern for what the life of a saint looks like. Contrary to our attempts to legislate holiness through the imposition of Victorian-era morality and assert our human control over how God works in the world, God meets each of us where we are and from that flawed, eccentric, and all-too-human mix of wheat and chaff draws us out of ourselves and into the love of Christ.

As the lives of the saints certainly attest, being a saint in one area of one's life doesn't mean that one is without faults and flaws in other areas of their messy human lives. Saints, as theologian Rowan Williams says, are people who are willing to stand in the light and let the light of God shine through. He continues, "Alleluia for saints, for saints who are ready to carry the cost of standing in the light, even when the light shows up their own inadequacies and oddities." And so it is not the particular attributes or behaviors of the saints that we must strive to emulate as if holiness were a type of Miss Manners guidebook to the spiritual life; that would be mere legalism after all. The light of God shining through the broken glass of our lives manifests in all sorts of different ways. Indeed, God seems to delight in the teeming diversity of the expression of holiness. Our God is not a God of cookie cutters and abstract ideals. Rather, in baptism, God works through the Spirit with our unique individual character and personal history to make manifest God's love in and for the world. So with Lazarus, may each of us heed the megaphone call to new life in Christ and learn to let go of those funeral cloths that bind us to a life of isolation, loneliness, and self-concern. May we, with all our foibles and quirks, learn to see those places in our lives, and in the lives of those around us, where God's light shines through.

You might be thinking, "That was the sermon—wow, that was short! Where is this church?" I edited Reverend Tyler's words to provide enough context around the message I thought was so compelling. You can apply these words to your own life in a way that helps your connection to and conversations with God, but if that's not for you, there are some pretty major life lessons wrapped up in this powerful message too.

Here are a few that stood out to me:

"For, in the final analysis, saints aren't the kind of people who live out a 'ten-point plan to holiness' and hold to a rigid set of rules. There is no one pattern for what the life of a saint looks like." There isn't a pattern for what the life of a saint looks like, or the life of a minimalist, or the life of a deeply soulful person. We get to be who we are. We can stop comparing, measuring up, and trying to prove our worth by emulating some version of ourselves that we think people expect us to be. For instance, I've incorporated minimalism and simplicity into my life in a way that resonates with my heart, and my family. It supports

love and health in my life. I created a lifestyle that is meaningful to me so it doesn't matter what other people think, or if I change my mind about any part of it. It doesn't matter if I follow a specific plan, own a certain number of items, or keep things others may not. I know what matters. This is my soulful simplicity.

"Saints are people who are willing to stand in the light and let the light of God shine through." When we show up and stand in the light, flaws and all, we get the opportunity to shine, to share our story, to show the world who we are. And we give others like us a chance to say "me too."

"May we learn to let go of those funeral cloths that bind us to a life of isolation, loneliness, and self-concern. May we, with all our foibles and quirks, learn to see those places in our lives, and in the lives of those around us, where God's light shines through." When we let go of the stuff that binds us, we will be free. If we keep shedding layers of the meaningless stuff, and other things that keep us in the dark, we will reveal our souls to ourselves and others. Keep letting go and let the light shine through.

"As the lives of the saints certainly attest, being a saint in one area of one's life doesn't mean that one is without faults and flaws in other areas of their messy human lives." We are never going to get it all right. When one part of our life is thriving, another may be suffering. We can't wait until we've got it all figured out, until we are flaw-free, to be ourselves and share our stories. We have to share from the mess because it will always be messy.

Less shiny, more real.
Less show, more soul.
Less perfection, more light.

If we want the light to shine through, we have to show up with our flaws and messy lives and stand in the light.

CHAPTER THIRTY-SIX

A Simple Life
Is Not the End Goal

When I decided to quit stress as a way to heal, I didn't plan to simplify my life. I didn't plan to give away most of my stuff, quit my job, sell my house, or narrow my wardrobe down to thirty-three items. Simplicity wasn't the plan. There was no plan. All I wanted to do was get better. It started with a small change to my diet. Once the diet felt like the new normal, I moved on to the next sources of stress: clutter, then debt.

A soulful simplicity is not about living with the least amount of stuff, meditating the longest, or being in a competition in any sense of the imagination. Sometimes simplicity and other major life changes look like that on Facebook or other social media streams, or even in our own minds, but really it's about you—your heart, your soul, your life. What works for you may not work for someone else. There isn't one solution. With all of the focus on minimalism, simplicity, decluttering, and capsule wardrobes, it's easy to believe that a simple life is the dream, but a simple life is not the end goal. We don't remove the clutter, reduce the stress, and boycott busyness to have a simple life. *We do it to have a life.*

When we are constantly defeated by not being simple enough or decluttered enough, we lose sight of what we are really after. We simplify to have a life full of the things that really matter to us. For me, that means a life of purpose, connection, contribution, adventure, laughter, early mornings, quiet evenings, and love. Your list may look a little different but when you are engaged in the things that light you up, it's easier to let go of the things that don't, including perfection and comparison.

The next time you are done paying off a credit card or cleaning out your closet, or completing whatever simplicity step you are on, stop. Before simplifying further, think about what you really want out of this life of yours. Is this the time to simplify more, or is this the time to deepen a connection with someone you love? Is this the time to move on to your bookshelves, or is this the time to create something new or serve in your community? Perhaps it is simply time to rest.

Simplifying with the goal of becoming as simple as possible will prove to be as empty as changing your diet to be as skinny as possible. It's not satisfying and it never lasts. As you create more time, energy, space, and attention in your life, use the simplicity to make a life you are excited to wake up to every day. Use it to better engage in relationships. Use it to instill confidence to live where you want, work where you want, and most important, to finally be who you are.

When decluttering is frustrating, or you regret spending too much, or you aren't sure where this whole simplicity journey is headed, remind yourself that you aren't creating a simple life, you are making a life.

CHAPTER THIRTY-SEVEN

Simplicity Is the Way Back to Love

Simplicity has been the way back to people I love, work I love, and a life that makes me smile at least ninety-nine times a day. On your soulful simplicity journey, look for love along the way. It may be hard to see it in the beginning, especially if you are worried about how far you have to go, or if you are afraid to change. Keep looking. Notice love in ordinary moments and motions. It will become easier to see the love you are making as you create more time and space.

It may start with decluttering your kitchen. Once you clear the clutter in your kitchen, simplicity shines a light on your kitchen table and the meals you used to share there before you covered it with bills, schoolwork, and the other things that had no place of their own. The clutter-free table is your way back to healthy meals, family laughter, and candlelit romantic dinners. It's your way back to love.

Simplicity may start in your closet. At first, the focus is on sorting and donating clothes, but after a while, your lighter wardrobe attracts more compliments, less decision fatigue, and the happy realization that you are wearing your favorite clothes every day. You stop wearing the jeans that pinch your waist, the coat you wore during a bad relationship, and the shoes you held on to because they were so expensive, even though they give you blisters. You get rid of the guilt, the sadness, and all the other emotions tied up in your clothes, and find your way back to love.

If you've been holding on to things that support activities you've enjoyed over the years, you might have several collections of sporting equipment, craft supplies, journals, hiking gear, video games, and other things, but not enough time or attention to engage in those activities. Maybe you fell out of love with camping or jewelry making, or forgot how much you loved it. Let go of the stuff that represents your past: the tent you never use, the tandem bike your partner refuses to ride, or boxes of things you are saving *just in case*. Choose one activity that makes you smile and find your way back to love. Do you have lots of great ideas and passion projects that you never start or finish? What can you cut to make room for your best work? Is there one project you can choose to move forward with right now, while you put the rest on the back burner? The love may fade for the ones you set aside, but then you can pour all the love into one. Work on something that makes your heart sing and you will find your way back to love.

If you push and struggle to be happy, and feel like you have to keep seeking and proving, or if perfection and comparison stand between you and joy, confidence, or hope, there is a simple way to get back to love. Go outside, notice the clouds, walk around the lake, or take a few deep breaths in the park. Nature will remind you that you are enough and that you deserve to find your way back to love.

As you simplify your calendar, and start saying no when your heart says no, you will have more time to take care of yourself, think, and linger. Most mornings, I don't check e-mail, I don't work on work, and I don't clean my house. Usually, the only thing I work on in the morning is my heart, and I'm okay with that. Let go of what you think you should do, work on your heart, and you will find your way back to love.

CHAPTER THIRTY-EIGHT

A Different Kind of More

She was all that mattered. I was deeper in debt, legal fees, and uncertainty than ever before, but I held on tight to my vow to give her more. I would give her everything. I'd work harder, make more, buy her more, do more for her, and prove to her that everything would be okay. I had no idea that this new goal would be just as damaging, and just as hard on my heart. My desire to give my daughter more wasn't wrong, just misguided. While I could never have articulated it then, I did want more for both of us, but not more stuff and money. What I wanted was more love, connection, laughter, and adventure, but that was too hard to measure. Instead, I made more money, worked more, spent more, and accumulated more. Living with less opened the door to a different kind of more: more space, more time, more light, more freedom, and yes . . . more love.

It has always been about love. My mom showered me with love on our trips to Boston, and I went into debt loving my three-year-old with Christmas presents she could never appreciate. All of the more . . . it wasn't just for Bailey. It was for me too because I didn't just think more + more = more, I thought more + more = love. By letting go, I was able to see that love could stand alone. It didn't have to come attached to presents, shopping trips, or big work bonuses or acknowledgments. I didn't have to earn or prove love. When I got rid of the stuff, the debt, the busyness, and the distractions that were swallowing me, I was surrounded by love. It was everywhere.

> *I had enough.*
> *I am enough.*
> *I don't need more approval.*
> *I don't need more money and stuff.*
> *I don't need more anymore.*

When I discovered that I was enough without anything else, I saw that I was love. I am love. You are too. We've been the love we seek all along. It's just been hiding beneath all of the layers of clutter, busyness, and show we use to protect ourselves from the pain.

Diamonds Are Not This Girl's Best Friend

Diamonds are not my best friend but they used to be. It wasn't just jewelry but all the things I bought to lift me up, prove my worth, and demonstrate my love. As I became more and more me and started experiencing the world from this new stuff-less place, I realized that diamonds are not this girl's best friend. My best friend is a magical rooftop sunrise. My best friend is the ocean. My best friend is a hike in the mountains. My best friend is a peaceful afternoon. My best friend is a really good book. My best friend is laughter. My best friend is seeing the world. My best friend is time with people I love. Diamonds have nothing on my best friends.

So yes, I want more, but not more stuff. I want more early mornings, more hiking and connecting with nature, more meaningful conversations and hand holding. More seeing the world. More creativity. More crazy ideas. More love. Always more love.

With a soulful simplicity and living with less, my life has become more than I ever imagined. Instead of more money, more stuff, more busyness, and more stepping outside of myself to be who other people may need me to be, I'm enjoying a different kind of more. I am more myself and more connected to my heart. I am more available for people I love and projects I care about. I'm more present and focused. I have more space, time, and love in my life along with all of the other mores I craved for so long.

I am always learning something new about how simplicity works on my heart, changes my relationships, and influences my work. At first my journey was focused on tasks like decluttering, paying off debt, and downsizing. The changes started on the outside while the real work was happening on the inside. With each thing, obligation, or assumption I let go of, I remembered who I was. I saw how far I had strayed and made it a priority to come back to myself. Forgetting who you are and living outside of your heart is painful. Do whatever it takes to come back and be more you. Give yourself all the space, time, and love you need to remember who you are.

CHAPTER THIRTY-NINE

Calling All Graceful Stumblers

It might seem that because I wrote a book, I have everything figured out, but the truth is that I am usually stumbling through. There are times when

I don't feel qualified to run my own business

I don't know if I can write something meaningful

I don't treat people I love the way they deserve to be treated

I eat things that don't agree with me

I skip working out or meditating

I feel a little lost

While perfection has never been my goal, I'm not even close. I stumble even more when I'm not honest with myself, when I try to force something to work, or when I approach things in a way that is not congruent with my values. When I get frustrated and wish I did have it all figured out, I remember that the messiest times in my life have inspired the most profound change. In the middle of a mess, whether a health crisis, money problem, crumbling relationship, or moment of great uncertainty, it's hard to see the light. When will it end? What's on the other side? Sometimes, until we have clarity, we get caught up in the drama, pain, or guilt and regret that often comes as a result. So yes, messes are painful, but they are also valuable. Getting through a mess provides confidence. You learn that you are strong and resilient, and that this too shall pass. Getting through one mess removes some of the mystery and drama from the next one. Sometimes it takes a big, heart wrenching mess to wake us up, inspire change, and to finally release us from the guilt of getting there in the first place. When our imperfections are splattered all over the floor, it becomes clear that we had to go through them to get to the lessons, the healing, and the enormous blessings.

We can look back at past relationships with people, money, stuff, and time with guilt, blame, and regret but to what end? How can we love ourselves for who we are when we hate ourselves for what we did? And if we don't love who we are, how does that help us love the amazing people in our lives today? How will it help us treat the precious time we have now with more purpose and intention? Before we can fix a problem we have to see it. For example, if you created a mess of your health because of how you treated your body, or a mess of your finances because of nonstop spending, or a mess of your love story because you treated someone poorly, acknowledge it. See it. Really see it.

Once we see it, we have a choice. We can become embroiled in guilt and perpetuate the mess and the pain or we can say, "This happened and now I am going to change." That doesn't mean we fix the past, but we find hope and healing today and tomorrow through change and growth. If the guilt and regret of past messes is standing between you and change, let go. Do whatever it takes to let it go. Release the pain by writing it down, by apologizing to people you hurt, or by sending those apologies to the heavens, universe, or the sea. And then forgive yourself. Forgiveness starts with you and is often step one in letting go of the emotional clutter you've been carrying. Start over knowing you and the people around you deserve better. Replace your guilt with gratitude.

If you are stumbling too, don't be hard on yourself. Instead stumble through with grace. Be curious and approach things with a beginner's mind. Keep things simple by eliminating excess drama, fear, and worry. Smile and breathe. Even though you can't see the finish line, everything is going to be okay. Enjoy the view. Look around as you are stumbling through. The end result may be where you have your sights set but the people you meet along the way and the lessons that present themselves are an important part of the journey. Keep forgiving. You are going to keep making mistakes not because you are flawed, but because you are human. Ask for help. Work with people who are willing to stumble through with you. My greatest teachers are always learning and willing to admit they don't have it all figured out either. Put your hands on your heart and keep coming back to you.

Anyone who tells you they have all the answers is lying. If we want to learn, love, grow, and thrive, we need fewer experts and more graceful stumblers. Let's put our expert/guru caps aside and stumble through gracefully together.

CHAPTER FORTY

Put Your Hands on Your Heart

If you are struggling to sit still, or the heart practice isn't resonating, forget about how you think you are supposed to do this. Forget about the instructions I gave you. Change things to create an environment where you can listen and connect. Try sitting in your favorite chair, lie in bed (unless you are really sleepy), or lie on a blanket on the floor with your legs up the wall. If it feels like talking to your heart is silly, talk to God, Buddha, the Universe, your intuition, or whomever or whatever you feel connected to. Don't be afraid to experiment and change things up. It might be just what you need to really get started. Once you create a comfortable place to start the conversation, your practice will grow. Find solace in the simple action of placing one hand over the other on your heart. "I've got you. I honor you. I trust you. I'm listening."

Suggested Questions for Making Love

Do I love myself? Talk about why or why not. If the answer is yes, how do you love yourself? Are there small daily changes you could make to treat yourself more lovingly?

Do I try to prove my love through gifts or other material items? Are those gifts a replacement for spending time with people you love? Do they replace loving words or actions?

What is written on my heart? What are the people, pets, and memories you hold in your heart? If guilt, remorse, or other things that make you sad are written on your heart, can you finally let go? You decide what's written on your heart.

Am I shiny and admired, or real and loved? Am I more show or soul? Reflect on how you act at home, at work, or around different people. Are you putting on an act or showing up as you?

Why am I afraid to stand in the light? Think about the things that prevent you from standing in the light. What don't you want people to know about you? What would happen if they found out? Maybe they'll say "me too" and fall in love with you.

Are there people I spend time with in the name of love who don't treat me in a loving way? If you spend time with people who make you prove your worth, who hurt you physically or emotionally, or people who bring you down time and time again, begin to spend more time with those people who lift you up. Don't guilt yourself with shoulds and supposed-tos. You deserve better.

What can I let go of to make room for more love? Think about how you can encourage love in the time and space you are creating.

MAKING LOVE: ACTION STEPS

Work through this list in any order, trying one thing at a time.

Let go of the items you think other people may want someday. Instead of guessing, or assuming, ask them, "Do you want this?" If the answer is yes, give it to them. If the answer is no, let it go.

Enjoy your sentimental items. Find a few items that mean something to you and display them, use them, or like Krissy with her parent's handwritten words, keep them close to your heart.

Drop the act. Start to pay attention to how you act around different people and in different situations. When do you act less like you? Stop proving yourself or trying to make yourself fit in. Just be you.

Write your heart's mission statement. Include who you are, what you stand for, and what's important to you. Write it down and use it to remember your heart when you forget.

Build your decluttering muscles. Instead of letting go of the stuff that has a hold on your heart, start with the easy stuff and build strength.

Tell the story of your stuff. If you are only holding on to sentimental items for the memories, take a picture and write about the memory. Keep a digital folder for your sentimental stories and let the stuff go.

Take a victory lap. Give each item one last intentional, loving use and then say good-bye.

Stand in the light. Flaws, cracks, and all—get in the light. That's where the connection and the inspiration is. It's where you will begin to change the world.

Make a life that makes you smile at least ninety-nine times a day. Shift your focus from creating a simple life to making a life. Simplicity is just the tool; what you make with it is up to you.

Notice love in ordinary moments. You don't need to see stars to know you are in love. Look for it. It's everywhere.

Put your heart first. When you wake up in the morning, start with your heart. The e-mail, dishes, laundry, and everything else can wait. Put your hands on your heart, even if only for a few minutes, and remember who you are before you start your day.

Simplicity isn't about organized sock drawers and clean countertops, but instead it is the beginning of remembering yourself and it's your way back to love. So where do you start? Pick one of the action steps or other recommendations throughout this book. You can't pick wrong. None is more important than the others. How you start matters much less than that you do start. Put your soulful simplicity into action in the order that most speaks to your heart, the order that best serves your soul, your family, and your life.

Start here with your hands on your heart.

ACKNOWLEDGMENTS

This book wouldn't have happened without the support, encouragement, wisdom, and love from the following people.

To Wendy Sherman, my wonderful literary agent. I'm pretty sure we fell in love on our very first call together.

To Jonathan Fields, who introduced me to Wendy, and helped me in so many ways. I often think of your words from an e-mail you sent me before we even met, "I smile when you rise."

To my editor Sara Carder and her team at TarcherPerigee. Thanks for believing we could do this together.

To Jayme Johnson, for holding my hand in the book world.

To Heidi Larsen and Tessa Woolf, my besties and OFO girls who helped me escape from the corporate world, cheered me on through every crazy idea, celebrated every win with me, and never doubted I could write this book.

To my friends: Rachel Shanken, Diana Riser, Kellie Puckett, and Tammy Strobel. We don't see each other often, but when we do it's like we've never been apart. I thought of each of you so many times while writing this.

To my GLP immersion family and all of my yoga teachers, especially Jennifer Ellen Adamson-Hulse and Scott Moore. You didn't just teach me yoga poses, you taught me how to find my heart. So many of your lessons influenced this book.

To Anne Marie and David. Thank you for all of the time and miles you've put in on your bikes to raise money to end multiple sclerosis. I love you for fighting for me.

Thank you Brita, Paul, and Maureen for welcoming Bailey and me into your hearts from the moment we met. Love you all.

For every person who has considered if something I wrote resonated with their heart, shared one of my blog posts, liked a Facebook post, attended a Tiny Wardrobe Tour event, sent me a kind e-mail, grown up on the Internet with me, and become part of the Be More with Less community. I love you so much.

Thank you to my parents, Nancy and George, for all your love and support and for sharing Italy with me. Mom, you taught me how to travel and be curious about the world. Dad, you taught me how to appreciate rainbows and how to tow a Volvo with an MG. Love you both.

To my sister and friend Alyson Dopfer. Watching cows and climbing mountains in Germany with you, Andreas, Axel, and Alexa has become one of my favorite traditions. I've tried to infuse the slow down I felt there in the pages of this book. I love each of you so much.

And for my loves.

To Mark for loving and lifting me up through it all.

To Bailey. You mean everything to me. xo

COURTNEY CARVER launched her blog *Be More with Less* in 2010 and is one of the top bloggers in the world on the subject of minimalism. She has been featured in countless articles, podcasts, and interviews on simplicity and is the creator of the minimalist fashion challenge Project 333, which was featured in *O, The Oprah Magazine* and *Real Simple*.